Unlocking The E... Ephesians

2nd Edition

By

Joseph Gilson (BD)

Declaration

I certify that all the material in this work which is not my own is duly acknowledged.

Signature: …………………………..

All rights reserved, including the right to reproduce this book, or portions thereof in any form. No part of this text may be reproduced, transmitted, downloaded, decompiled, reverse engineered, or stored, in any form or introduced into any information storage and retrieval system, in any form or by any means, whether electronic or mechanical without the express written permission of the author.

ISBN: 9798494740632

Dedication page

This book is dedicated to all those who desire to deepen their understanding of scriptures and all those who would like to take time to reflect and debate on some questions of life.

Table of contents
1. Preface
2. Epigraph
3. Foreword
4. Introduction to the Book of Ephesians
5. The reason for Paul's incarceration
6. Paul's prison experience
7. Paul's different way of scripture interpretation
8. Muddiman's augment on Paul's way of writing
9. Postcolonial perspective of the book of Ephesians
10. The Ancient Ephesus
11. The hardships faced by the Church

12 Paul' third missionary journey.
13 Exposition of Ephesians 1:1.
14 Ephesians 1:2
15. Elaboration of Ephesians 1:3
16 Ephesians 1:4 -6.,
17 Ephesians 1:7-11
18. Eph 1:9-
19. Eph 1:13
20. Eph 1:15-17
21 Eph 1:17-23
22 Ephesians 2:1-3.
23 Ephesians 2:8-9.
24. Eph 2:11-16
25. Eph 2:17-22
26. Eph 2:18
27. Eph 2:20-22
28. Eph 3:1
29. Eph 3:3-7
30. Eph 3:8-9
31. Eph.3:10-11
32. Eph 3:12
33. Eph 3:13

34. Eph 3:14-17
35. Eph 3:18-19
35. Eph 3:20-21
36. Eph 4:1-2
37. Eph 4:3-6
38. Eph 4:7-12
39. Eph 4:13-16
40. Eph 4:17-23
41. Eph 4:24-28
42. Eph 4: 29
43. Eph 4:30
44. Eph 4:31
45. Eph 4:32
46. Eph 5:1
47. Eph 5:2
48. Eph 5:3-5
49. Eph 5:6-7
50. Eph 5:8:13
51. Eph 5:14-17
52. Eph 5:18-21
53. Eph 5:22-23
54. Eph 6:1-9
55. Eph 6:10-18
56. Eph 6:12
57. Eph 6:18-24
57. Conclusion
58. Acknowledgements
59. About the Author
60. Footnotes
61. Bibliography

Epigraph

"'I have a dream that my four little children will one day live in a nation where they will not be judged by the color of their skin but by the content of their character.'[1]
Martin Luther King Jr

---

[1] Pep Talk , *Master the Art of Public Speaking.* India.2020,35

Preface

The information contained in this book is presented to give an insight into social history and it's present. I aim to develop people's skills such as analytical and critical thinking in order to be able to analyse writing, arguments and concepts in an extensive range of contexts

Foreword

As a dear friend and colleague, I know Chaplain Joseph Gilson to be a conscientious and loving man who displays the compassion and grace the Son of God and our Lord Jesus Christ commissioned us to show one another.

Obtaining his BD degree in Theology and the challenges he faced as a young man growing up in Africa enables him to identify, minister and care for people from different spheres and ethnicity. With many years of Pastoral experience, and love for the Scriptural Truth of the Bible, Gilson furthermore, brings the message of hope to those in times of suffering and hopelessness during the unprecedented times of the Covid-19 pandemic.

Trinitarian Blessings
Sharon Connolly

Theological Studies BA (UHI)

Introduction

The book of Ephesians is one of Paul's prison epistles written from the Roman prison to the church of Ephesus in about A.D 62,63. This book is very different from all of Paul's books in that Paul doesn't seem to be addressing problems instead he appears to be elaborating on the Christian doctrines. It has become rare for many preachers not to correct the wrong in the Church each time they stand up to preach. Guzik asserts: 'Karl Marx wrote about a new man and a new society, but he saw man and society both in almost purely economic terms and offered only economic answers. In his letter to the Ephesians, Paul also saw the new man and a new society, but he saw it all accomplished by the work of Jesus.'[2] This explains that this book acts as a manual for the new man living in a new society that is accomplished by Jesus Christ as Paul teaches on various issues pertaining Christian life. It is a good attitude for the ministers of the gospel to train their minds to see the good which is in their congregations instead of seeing the bad that need to be corrected. This way of thinking will help preachers not only to preach on the judgement and condemnation instead they will begin to focus on the love and grace of God as Paul did. Pastor Joseph Prince is a good example of the preachers who choose not to dwell much on judgements instead Prince preaches more on the grace of God which result to the fast

---

[2] David Guzik(2021),(enduring Word Bible Commentary Philippians)(OnlineBible Commentary) Available: https://enduringword.com/bible-commentary/Ephesians-1/ Accessed 24/01/2021

growth of the Church. People begin to see God not as an angry and evil God who is after punishing people but God become a loving and forgiving God.

Zondervan affirms: 'Most of the teaching of the letter is positively presented and is not expressed with the kind of polemical tone that one finds, for example, in Galatians, Romans, or 2 Corinthians. Although Paul is deeply concerned about the moral behaviour of the readers of Ephesians, his motivation to write does not seem to be prompted by his becoming aware of particular moral lapses by individuals within the community, comparable to what we find in 1 Corinthians. Nor does he seem to be responding to a series of questions that the church is asking of him (as we find, for instance, in 1 Corinthians with the repeated περὶ δέ).'[3] This proves that in his writing Paul did not have a particular situation which he addressed but he was actually grounding his churches in the knowledge of a new life in Christ. . This is what the present needs; preachers who can take time to ground and equip them on how to become the acceptable body of capable of participating in the body of Christ in a positive way.

---

[3] Zondervan. *Ephesians*. (Grand Rapids: HarperCollins Christian Publishing. 2010.)33

The reason for Paul's incarceration and his prison experience

After his conversion to Christ the Apostle Paul specialised on the liberation theology. His lenience to Gentiles got him great opposition from the Jews who accused him of causing inconvenience throughout the Jewish community as Luke narrated in Ac 24:5 (BBE) 'For this man, in our opinion, is a cause of trouble, a maker of attacks on the government among Jews through all the empire, and a chief mover in the society of the Nazarenes'[4] This explains the extent of the opposition that Paul encountered due to his lenience to the none Jews. The Jews thought that Paul's different view of scriptures was actually a rebellion and cause for uprisings in the nation. Paul seems to have been advocating for that liberty to interpret the scriptures in anyhow. We are actually privileged to live in such a time as this when we have freedom to interpret scriptures according to our different perceptions.

---

[4] Acts 24:5

Paul's difference and the new forms of scripture interpretations

Aymer draws from Moore: 'Nowadays, many methods are available, and biblical critics have increasingly used interdisciplinary approaches and a combination of theories and methods, such as postmodern theory, postcolonial theory, and queer studies, for interpretation'[5] This explains that we are in such a time when scriptures are open to different interpretation. However Interpretation should be centred on the author's original intention of sense and not the reader. This may suggest getting into the author 'perspective, culturally, historically, grammatically, and the literary procedures and conventions the author was using.

Scripture interpretation must also be done according to the context of the passage of which the political situation can be a hindrance especially at this day and age where preachers like to remain within political correctness in order to gain favour of the government. As a result most preachers interpret a verse by itself in isolation without considering its context.

On the other way scripture interpretations should be determined by our sensitivity to differences between the church and the Hebrew Nation and New Covenant and Old Covenant requirements of which the Apostle Paul was very much aware of these differences.

---

[5] Margaret Aymer, Kittredge, Cynthia Briggs, and Sanchez, David A., eds. *The Letters and Legacy of Paul Fortress Commentary on the Bible.*)31

At times we might have to use the much clear scripture to interpret another passage of scripture. This explains the flexibility we should have in scripture interpretations.

It is because of his persistence in this kind of preaching that Paul is finally incarcerated in Roman prison an environment that was very conducive to be in. It is clear that Paul experienced a extensive selection of Roman prison circumstances. According to Acts 16:23-30 Paul was chained in a general holding cell in Philippi and later incarcerated in most likely better conditions in the praetorian at Caesarea according to Acts 23:35. We gather from Acts 28:30 that he might transferred the house arrest in Rome.

Paul was responsible for supporting himself regarding his food and clothing according to Acts 28:30. It is most likely that Paul depended on the income from his tent-making and members of his church including the Church of Philippi to which he sent a letter of appreciation through Epaphroditus. Paul was looked after by soldiers of the elite Praetorian Guard all the time.

Paul's plea to Caesar in Rome became the fulfilment of his desire to take the gospel of Christ to Rome as proclaimed by Luke : Ac 19:21(BBE) 'Now after these things were ended, Paul came to a decision that when he had gone through Macedonia and Achaia he would go to Jerusalem, saying, After I have been there, **I have a desire to see Rome**.'[6] Paul eagerly wanted to preach his message of salvation to both Jews and Gentiles although this was fulfilled in a different way from what he expected. At times God's answer to prayer comes in disguised form or in an unexpected way causing many to miss it out due to their spiritual insensitivity.

---

[6] Acts 19:21

Confirming his assignment to Rome, Paul had a vision: Ac 23:11 (BBE) 'And the night after, the Lord came to his side and said, Be of good heart, for as you have been witnessing for me in Jerusalem, **so will you be my witness in Rome.**' His petition to Caesar became an opportunity for Paul to fulfil his mission in Rome although this ushered himself at the disposal of Emperor Nero the most vicious tyranny who ceased an opportunity to eliminate Christianity from the outbreak of the fire. Lightfoot declares: 'The great fire which then devastated Rome became the signal for an onslaught on the innocent Christians; and one regarded as the ringleader of the hated sect could hardly have escaped the general massacre.'[7] This indicates that Paul became a target of the persecution as a ringleader of Christians who were being accused of causing the great fire which shattered Rome. This explains how unbearable the conditions the Roman prison in which Paul found himself in yet Paul ceased an opportunity of furthering the gospel of salvation in Rome.

Spencer asserts: 'No clear traditions recount exactly where in Rome Paul was being held during the writing of this last letter. Probably, not under house arrest, yet not at the Mamertine dungeon (where any writing would be impossible), he may have been incarcerated in a military camp or palace in the city, bound to a soldier, as had been Agrippa.'[8] Referring to the situation in the dungeon where there was no light and packed out with other prisoners, it could have been very difficult for Paul to attain a pure concentration of thought as he wrote his epistles. Paul must have been so much dedicated to his work of writing

---

[7] B.Lightfoot, J.. *Philippians*. Wheaton: Crossway. 1994)15

[8] Aida Spencer Besançon. *2 Timothy and Titus*. (Eugene: Wipf and Stock Publishers. 2014.)76

utilising every opportunity he found while he was in that unbearable situation.

Muddiman's augment on Paul's way of writing

Segovia asserts: 'In such a recent commentary as John Muddiman's, it is a bit shocking to see a scholar dismiss the possibility that Ephesians was written to counter political propaganda or state persecution.'[9] This evidences the fact that Paul wrote this letter to the believers of Ephesus to counter the state persecution and the political propaganda within the Roman Empire.

Postcolonial perspective of the book of Ephesians

On a postcolonial perspective of the book of Ephesians Segovia draws from Perkins: 'Admittedly almost ten years old now, this quotation from Pheme Perkins' work reflects the trend within scholarship that replicates the escapism into the 'spiritual' realm that is contained within Ephesians itself: 'Some have even compared [the language about God's plan for humanity in this letter] to claims for the peace created by the Roman Empire. Though there is no clear evidence that Ephesians is concerned with imperial ideology, the suggestion points to

---

[9]Segovia, Fernando F., and Sugirtharajah, R. S., eds. *A Postcolonial Commentary on the New Testament Writings : Postcolonial Commentary on the New Testament Writings*. (London: Bloomsbury Publishing Plc.2009)274

the spiritual importance of its message' (1997: 32). I do not wish to indict Perkins' opinions and work. On the contrary, I respectfully draw upon her work, intending to highlight how deeply rooted the preference for a spiritualized interpretation is for many scholars.'[10] This suggests reading the message of the book in its literal meaning in relation to the Roman Empire Politics rather than spiritualising its meaning. We might need to consider the general or plain meaning of the text. Segovia further declares: 'However, even as I make such a declaratory statement, I am aware that many well-intentioned scholars continue to resist or deny the importance of applying a postcolonial interpretation. This resistance indicates not only the extent to which biblical studies, as generally taught or conceived within many Western locations, is apolitical and thus has lost a significant aspect of the texts' originating impetus, but also the extent to which depoliticizing the biblical texts serves to maintain instead of transform the status quo.'[11] Again this gives us an idea that the Roman colonization might have been of great influence to the writing of this letter to the Ephesians. This explains how most scholars try to rule out the politic influence on the writing of certain scriptures. I personally think that Paul being born from Tarsus which was once a Roman colony although it was now independent at the time of Paul's birth, Therefore Paul might have been influenced by his geographical and political location just I personal was influenced by the social environment around

---

[10]Segovia, Fernando F., and Sugirtharajah, R. S., eds. *A Postcolonial Commentary on the New Testament Writings : Postcolonial Commentary on the New Testament Writings.* (London: Bloomsbury Publishing Plc.2009)265

[11]Segovia, Fernando F., and Sugirtharajah, R. S., eds. *A Postcolonial Commentary on the New Testament Writings : Postcolonial Commentary on the New Testament Writings.* 266

me during the *Black lives matter protests* as I wrote my book on *Equality In Diversity.*

West affirms : 'Despite the substantial interest in postcolonialism and postcolonial biblical criticism in many parts of the world, (South) African biblical scholarship has been cautious in its response.'[12] This explains the colonial influence in the Biblical interpretation in South Africa. South Africa experienced great apartheid which resulted to the imprisonment of Nelson Mandela for 37 years. It becomes difficult not to reference the scriptures to such a dominant situation in South Africa.

The Ancient Ephesus

Ephesus was an olden Greek city on the coast of Ionia, three kilometres southwest of present-day Selçuk in İzmir Province, Turkey. It was constructed on a river bend, that was eventually rummaged into a full harbor near the mount of the Cayster River, on the western coast of Asia Minor (modern Turkey). Along the seashore between Smyrna to the north and Miletus to the south, the site is now about six miles from the Aegean Sea. It was the most important trading centre within the Mediterranean region. During Paul's time Ephesus was also very popular for Idol worship. DeSilva asserts: ' The goddess worshipped there was after all, Diana/Artemis of Ephesus as attested not only by the record of Acts 19:28, 34 but by many provincial and civic coin mintings that celebrated Diana

---

[12] West, G. O. (2008). DOING POSTCOLONIAL BIBLICAL INTERPRETATION @HOME: TEN YEARS OF (SOUTH) AFRICAN AMBIVALENCE. *Neotestamentica, 42*(1), 147–164.
http://www.jstor.org/stable/43049259 accessed: 11/10/21

Ephesia on their reverses.'[13] This gives an impression that people of Ephesus worshipped Diana as their goddess of which statures and temples were built in the name of this cult. This may highlight Paul's aim to divert people from idolatry to the worship of the God Almighty. It was in Ephesus that Paul challenged idolatry and burned the silversmith's books resulting to a riot against him. Anthony affirms: 'Luke records great success in Ephesus, including the burning of books on magic. He also recounts the minor riot of silversmiths, who accused Paul of damaging their trade and the reputation of Ephesus (Acts 19.23– 41). Paul left Ephesus for Macedonia, exercising pastoral care for three months (Acts 20.1– 3).'[14] This indicates that Paul was not afraid of any opposition that he encountered along his missionary way. He might actually have enjoyed facing challenges. Just as aerobic exercise repeatedly may toughen heart and lungs and improve blood circulation, which can help the development of stamina so is the spiritual warfare as it build endurance.

The hardships faced by the Church

Osborne affirms: 'There was also a strong Jewish presence in the city. While the Romans generally allowed the Jews to practice their religion freely, there is evidence of persecution and disfavor in Ephesus and the region. This is reflected in persecution against the church, which was initially assumed by the Romans to have been a Jewish sect. This situation of pressure and oppression

---

[13] David A Desilva. A Week in the life of Ephesus. InterVarsity Press Downers Grove, Illinois. 2020) 32
[14] Anthony Thiselton *The Living Paul : An Introduction to the Apostle's Life and Thought.* (Downers Grove: InterVarsity Press. 2010.)32

continued into the 90s, as seen in the book of Revelation.'[15] This indicates the opposition that Paul and the church faced from the Roman government as some historians records Christians dying through burning or even given to fight against the wild animals like lions. The Church persecution continues even to this twenty first century where in over 50 countries it is dangerous to be a follower of Christ especially in Nigeria.

Paul' third missionary journey

Drawing from the works of Anthony: 'We know, however, that Paul spent three years of hard toil at Ephesus, from where he undertook short journeys to proclaim the gospel and to strengthen the churches.'[16] This shows that Paul used Ephesus his base for reaching out to other Churches in Asia Minor. Anthony further asserts: 'Towards the close of this period of the so-called third missionary journey, Paul indicated that he had now planted the gospel in strategic centres of Asia Minor (especially Ephesus), Macedonia (especially Thessalonica), and Greece proper (especially Corinth) (Rom. 15.19, 23). His eyes now looked towards Italy and Rome, and even beyond it to Spain (Rom. 15.23– 24; 16.28). He would carry the gospel westward, using Rome as his 'base', as Ephesus had been for Asia Minor.'[17] This indicates that Paul was following a well- planned strategy in his missionary work. For Paul to reach out to Rome he

---

[15] Osborne, Grant R. *Ephesians Verse by Verse*. Oak Harbor: Lexham Press.2017)10

[16] Anthony Thiselton C *The Living Paul : An Introduction to the Apostle's Life and Thought*. (Downers Grove: InterVarsity Press. 2010.)33

[17]Anthony Thiselton *(The Living Paul : An Introduction to the Apostle's Life and Thought.)*34

had to go through Jerusalem where he was going to be arrested and use the opportunity as a prisoner to preach in Rome. Anthony declares: 'Paul preached in Troas, and after stopping in Lesbos sailed to Mytilene and then to Miletus. The elders from Ephesus met him, and he preached his farewell sermon to them. We cannot think of Paul as a harsh and insensitive controversialist or misogynist when we read that (according to Luke), 'There was much weeping . . . they embraced Paul and kissed him, grieving . . . that they would not see him again' (Acts 20.37– 38).'[18] Having caused a riot from the silversmiths in Ephesus Paul had to meet the elders of the church of Ephesus at Miletus. It looks like Paul was not even surprised by Agabus's prophesy that Paul was going to be arrested in Jerusalem as highlighted by Luke in Acts 21:4-11 .As followers of Christ the Holy Spirit is available to encourage us as we may be suffering for the cause of Christ so it was with the Apostle Paul and even with Christ himself.

Exposition of Ephesians 1:1

Ephesians 1:1 (BEB) 'Paul, an Apostle of Christ Jesus by the purpose of God, to the saints who are at Ephesus, and those who have faith in Christ Jesus' Paul begins his writing in a defensive way proclaiming his apostleship of Jesus Christ not by human appointment but through the will of God. It is as if Paul's apostleship faced rejection or opposition, Therefore Paul had to defend it. It could be because Paul did not physically walk with Jesus as did the other twelve apostles. Elmer draws from Bruce : ' 'There may also be here, as F. F. Bruce points out, a further implied charge that Paul had failed to preach that gospel

---

[18]Anthony Thiselton (*The Living Paul : An Introduction to the Apostle's Life and Thought.*)35

correctly, abridging and adulterating the import of the message that he had received at Jerusalem."[19] This means that the Judaisers were accusing Paul of misrepresenting Jewish authority in his missionary work by disregarding the Law of Moses; as a result they questioned his Apostleship. That's the reason Paul had to defend his Apostleship in most of his salutation to the Church of Ephesus. Having known that his apostleship was not acceptable to the Jews in Jerusalem Paul had to be specific in his salutation about his apostleship to the saints in Ephesus.

Williamson asserts: 'Paul briefly introduces himself and salutes his readers with his customary greeting. The word apostle comes from the Greek verb "to send" and means someone who has been "sent" as an official representative. Paul refers to the one who sent him by his title, Christ Jesus. Just as Jesus' appointment of the Twelve was in accord with the will of the Father— it followed a night of prayer (Luke 6:12– 13)—so Paul's appointment as the †Messiah's authorized delegate (Acts'[20] This indicates that although Paul did not walk with Jesus directly as the other twelve apostles, on his way to Damascus to persecute the Christians, Paul had an encounter with Jesus Christ who assigned him with the work of an apostle. The Jews had the right to question his apostleship as they did not experience Paul's experience with Jesus Christ.

Drawing from the works of Moule ,Guzik asserts: '**To the saints who are in Ephesus**: In a few ancient manuscripts there is a blank space instead of the words in

---

[19]Elmer, Ian J. *Paul, Jerusalem and the Judaisers : The Galatian Crisis in Its Broadest Historical Context.*(Mohr Siebeck, Tübingen,2009)2
[20] Williamson, Peter S.. *Ephesians*. (Grand Rapids: Baker Academic.2009)41

Ephesus. Based partly on this, some believe that this letter was actually a circular letter written not to any one congregation, but meant to be passed on to many different congregations in different cities.'[21] This may mean that Paul intended to instruct some of his churches too including the church of Ephesus. This may indicate that many churches at that time were be facing similar challenges of which it would save Paul some time to use the same template to address all his churches instead of writing the new one. This indicates that all scripture is useful and applicable to all many different audiences. Paul affirms that in 2Tim3:16,17(KJV) 'All scripture is given by inspiration of God, and is profitable for doctrine, for reproof, for correction, for instruction in righteousness: That the man of God may be perfect, thoroughly furnished unto all good works.'[22] This may indicate that Paul might have used the same epistles to address different churches just as the same antibiotic may be effective for different infections in the body so is the word of God (scripture). Zondervan affirms: 'In recent years, some scholars have contended that this high degree of similarity is a sign of literary borrowing, namely, that the author of Ephesians has used Colossians as a literary source. Proponents of this view argue that the author of Ephesians was not slavishly dependent on Colossians, but rearranged and gave fresh expression to his source material to suit his own independent theological purposes.'[23] This reveals that the scholars in recent years disputed the point that Paul used

---

[21] David Guzik(2021),(enduring Word Bible Commentary Ephesians)(OnlineBible Commentary) Available: https://enduringword.com/bible-commentary/Ephesians-1/ Accessed 24/01/2021

[22] 2Timothy 3:16,17

[23] Zondervan. *Ephesians.* (2010)42

the same letter of Ephesians to address some of his churches.

Ephesians 1:2

Ephesians 1:2 (BBE) 'Grace to you and peace from God our Father and the Lord Jesus Christ'[24] It may appear as if Paul missed the mention of the Holy Spirit which may be misjudged as if Paul disregarded the trinity in the mention of the father and the son only. In actual fact Paul was a strong believer in the Trinity probably with the understanding that Holy Spirit is already within the father and the son as they the three cannot be separated. Paul begins by declaring grace before getting into the essence of his letter. Elaborating on the meaning of grace Johnson draws from the evangelical dictionary of Theology: 'God's unlimited kindness toward his people regardless of what they might deserve. Christians often use the term as shorthand for the gospel, which is "the good news of God's grace" (Acts 20:24) or simply "the word of his grace" (Acts 20:32). This link between grace and the gospel indicates that the content of God's grace ultimately is identical to the relationship that God establishes with his people in and through Jesus Christ. As the eternal Son of God incarnate, Jesus reveals the true meaning of God's grace and is the one through whom it is distributed (John 1:14, 16).'[25] In the word grace Paul appears to be praying

---

[24] Ephesians 1:2
[25] Johnson, K.L. (2017). Grace. In W.A. Elwell, Evangelical dictionary of theology. (3rd ed.). [Online]. Ada: Baker Publishing Group.

for the church of Ephesus that they may experience the unconditional favour of God that came in the person of Christ. General speaking, after the fall, human kind deserved God's punishment but through his gracious attribute God offered Jesus Christ as atonement for the sins. Paul mentions the grace which is the undeserved or unmerited favour of God. Paul had an understanding of how imperfect human beings are and that we are only saved because of the grace of God rather than our own goodness. Paul declares in Ephesians 2:9 (CEV) 'It is not something you have earned, so there is nothing you can brag about.'[26] Paul acknowledges the human limitations to the required standards of holiness. This means that it is the grace of God, (unmerited favor) which qualifies us for the purposes of God.

For every instruction he was about to give them Paul lays a foundation of the grace of God as a point of reference. Furthermore Paul appears to be using the Jewish way of salutation by proclaiming peace (Shalom) from the Father and the lord Jesus Christ. Jesus also spoke peace as he entered the room John affirms: 'And after eight days the disciples were inside again, and Thomas was with them. Jesus came, the doors being shut, and stood in the midst and said, Peace to you!'[27] This indicates that it was the custom of Jesus to proclaim peace on arrival before venturing deep into the conversation as Paul does in his introduction of his letter.

Available from:
https://dtl.idm.oclc.org/login?url=https://search.credoreference.com/content/entry/bpgugxt/grace/0?institutionId=8909 [Accessed 28 January 2021].
[26] Ephesians 2:9
[27] John 20:26

Elaboration of Ephesians 1:3

Ephesians 1:3 The Passion Translation 'Every spiritual blessing in the heavenly realm has already been lavished upon us as a love gift from our wonderful heavenly Father, the Father of our Lord Jesus—all because he sees us wrapped into Christ. This is why we celebrate him with all our hearts!'[28] This is an indication that Paul was exhorting the church of Ephesus to start experiencing and living the new life of the kingdom of God rather than waiting to experience it in the eschatological future. The King James Version pronounces a blessing to God who had blessed his people with every spiritual blessings in heavenly places of which I wonder if the lesser can be in a position to offer a blessing to the superior of which humans are in this case being the lesser and God being the superior just as Abraham was blessed by Melchizedek in Genesis 14:17-20 and Jacob blessed his sons in Genesis 49. If that being the case the subjects or the lesser can only acknowledge the greatness of God instead of claiming to make God great or to bless him. Thielman asserts: 'The benediction, or berekah, has been for centuries the most common form of Jewish prayer and central to the piety of devout Jewish living. Long before the first century, Jews used both lengthy benedictions in corporate worship and brief benedictions in daily life as a way of praising God for various gracious gifts (Dahl 2000: 279– 308).'[29] This shows that the benediction or berekah did not belittle God instead it was a way of worshiping God. So everyone should bless God as a way of acknowledging his supremacy as David declared to himself: 'Psalms 103:1,2 (KJV) 'Bless the Lord, O my soul: and all that is within

---

[28] Eph 1:3 (The Passion Translation)
[29] Thielman, Frank. *Ephesians (Baker Exegetical Commentary on the New Testament).* (Grand Rapids: Baker Academic.2010)37

me, bless his holy name. Bless the Lord, O my soul, and forget not all his benefits.'[30]

Thielman goes on proclaiming: 'The centrality of the benediction to common Jewish piety in antiquity is also clear from the Mishnah's tractate Berakot (Benedictions), which is, significantly, the first tractate of the Mishnah's first order. Although this tractate is difficult to date, some of its details and much of its spirit probably originated before the destruction of the temple in AD 70. 1 The tractate provides instructions for saying the regular prayers of Judaism as well as prayers over meals and occasional, spontaneous prayers. 2 The benediction ("Blessed are you, O Lord, who . . .") is the common thread that binds all these prayers together. Some form of the Eighteen Benedictions was to be said three times a day (4.1, 3), prayers over meals took the form of benedictions (6– 8), and even the morning and evening confessions of the Shema were to be preceded and concluded with benedictions (1.4). Various events in the daily routine of life were also to be greeted by blessing God: passing by a place where God had worked a miracle for Israel (9.1), seeing a display of God's power in the natural world such as a thunderstorm (9.2), finishing construction on a house (9.3), and entering or leaving a town (9.4). Paul gives evidence in his letters of how integral such expressions of praise were to the life of a devout Jew (Rom. 1:25; 9:5; 2 Cor. 11:31).[31] This indicates that during the 2nd century It was saying the benediction at the for front of every conversation was a common practice as it gave all the praise to God as the giver of that particular thing. This is a great lesson even to this generation to acknowledge the

---

[30] Psalms 103:1,2
[31] Thielman, Frank. *Ephesians (Baker Exegetical Commentary on the New Testament.*2010).37-38.

Divine intervention beyond our human wisdom. With reference to the discovery of the new vaccines against the Covid 19, Scientists should not take credit but to acknowledge God's wisdom in it.

Williamson proclaims: 'Rather than referring to God as "King of the Universe" or "the God of Israel," as Jewish blessings typically do, this blessing identifies God as the "Father" of our Lord Jesus Christ (as in 2 Cor 1:3 and 1 Pet 1:3). Ever since Jesus' death and resurrection, Christians cannot think about God apart from Jesus or about Jesus except as God's Son.'[32] Paul clarifies on the controversy which was going during that time as the Jews doubted the deity of Jesus Christ as the son of God. Paul openly reveals that Jesus was the son of God.

Guzik proclaims: ' In ancient Greek (the language Paul originally wrote in), Ephesians 1:3 through 1:14 form one long sentence. As an opera has an overture, setting the tone for all the melodies that will follow, so Ephesians 1:3-14 sets the tone for the rest of Ephesians.'[33] This means that in these verses Paul is laying a foundation of his entire letter to the Ephesians.

The reason Paul blesses God is that God has already blessed us with all spiritual blessings in heavenly places. Guzik declares: 'The "us" includes both Jews and Gentiles in the church at Ephesus and beyond. It was important to point out that these blessings are for both Jewish and Gentile believers. First century Jews had a strong sense of

---

[32] Williamson, Peter S. *Ephesians*. (Grand Rapids: Baker Academic.2009)48
[33] David Guzik(2021),(enduring Word Bible Commentary Ephesians)(OnlineBible Commentary) Available: https://enduringword.com/bible-commentary/Ephesians-1/ Accessed 04/02/2021

being blessed, called, and predestined. Paul showed that these things are now given to Christians, be they Jew or Gentile.'[34] This is a call even for the present church to embrace the blessings which were claimed by the Jews or the Hebrew nation in the past but now we are all engrafted into the same kingdom of blessings. It takes a special revelation to understand that our visible world was formed from the invisible word of God and everything in the visible world begins in the spiritual invisible world. Whatever we may need in the visible world is already given in the spiritual invisible world and all we need is to imagine it and embrace it in the visible world as asserted by Paul: Ephesians 1:3 The Passion Translation 'Every spiritual blessing in the heavenly realm has already been lavished upon us as a love gift from our wonderful heavenly Father, the Father of our Lord Jesus—all because he sees us wrapped into Christ'[35]

Guzik draws from Spurgeon: '"We are not sitting here, and groaning, and crying, and fretting, and worrying, and questioning our own salvation. He has blessed us; and therefore we will bless him. If you think little of what God has done for you, you will do very little for him; but if you have a great notion of his great mercy to you, you will be greatly grateful to your gracious God." (Spurgeon)'[36] Spurgeon had a special revelation that we don't need to groan, cry, fret, and worry trying to beg God for the

---

[34] David Guzik(2021),(enduring Word Bible Commentary Ephesians)(OnlineBible Commentary) Available: https://enduringword.com/bible-commentary/Ephesians-1/ Accessed 04/02/2021

[35] Ephesians 1:3 (The Passion Translation)

[36] David Guzik(2021),(enduring Word Bible Commentary Ephesians)(OnlineBible Commentary) Available: https://enduringword.com/bible-commentary/Ephesians-1/ Accessed 04/02/2021

benefits of salvation which are already given instead we should embrace them and approach God in a thankful way. Paul indicates that all spiritual blessings are located in heavenly places where Christ sits. We might not see them with our physical eyes because they are located in heaven.

Guzik goes on drawing from Spurgeon who asserted that: '"Our thanks are due to God for all temporal blessings; they are more than we deserve. But our thanks ought to go to God in thunders of hallelujahs for spiritual blessings. A new heart is better than a new coat. To feed on Christ is better than to have the best earthly food. To be an heir of God is better than being the heir of the greatest nobleman. To have God for our portion is blessed, infinitely more blessed than to own broad acres of land. God hath blessed us with spiritual blessings. These are the rarest, the richest, the most enduring of all blessings; they are priceless in value." (Spurgeon)'[37] This explains that in heaven there is a store house of everything that may be needed in the physical world which we should be thankful to God for. Just as a car manufacture stores the parts of the car that he sells in case they have a break down, so is God the creator. It is not being a fanatic to claim the healing with the understanding that God can perform miracles by replacing the damaged part of our bodies with the perfect one from His store houses in heaven.

Guzik declares: 'If we have no appreciation for spiritual blessing, then we live at the level of animals. Animals live only to eat, sleep, entertain themselves, and to reproduce. We are made in the image of God and He

---

[37] David Guzik(2021),(enduring Word Bible Commentary Ephesians)(OnlineBible Commentary) Available: https://enduringword.com/bible-commentary/Ephesians-1/ Accessed 04/02/2021

has something much higher for us, yet many choose to live at the level of animals.'[38] This is a challenge to learn to appreciate the blessings we get from God on a daily basis. We might not be having all that we want but someone somewhere does not even have the little that we get.This explains that animals never appreciate but they only live to think about feeding and mating. When humans fail to give praise to God and only exist to feed and to make children they are lowering their standards to that of animals. It is through the atonement work of Christ that God gave us all these spiritual blessings. This means that as God was punishing sin through Christ the Church was in Christ. As we maintain our position in Christ we remain in a position of claiming all these benefits which belongs to Christ as he owns everything that belongs to God as the rightful beneficiary or heir of God's riches.

Ephesians 1:4 -6

Ephesians 1:4 -5(NKJV) 'according as He chose us in Him before the foundation of the world, that we should be holy and without blame before Him in love, having predestined us to the adoption of children by Jesus Christ to Himself, according to the good pleasure of His will,'[39] This introduces us to the subject of predestination. It means that no one is predestined to go to live a sinful life and to go to hell but that everyone was chosen by God to be holy and for eternal life. As a just God he gave each one of us a will to choose to do right or to do wrong. So it is our choice that we make that determines where we will

---

[38] David Guzik(2021),(enduring Word Bible Commentary Ephesians)(OnlineBible Commentary) Available: https://enduringword.com/bible-commentary/Ephesians-1/ Accessed 04/02/2021
[39] Ephesians 1:4-5(KJV)

spend out eternity whether in heaven or in Hell. Guzik draws from Calvin: 'We are chosen in Him. "For if we are chosen in Christ, it is outside ourselves. It is not from the sight of our deserving, but because our heavenly Father has engrafted us, through the blessing of adoption, into the Body of Christ. In short, the name of Christ excludes all merit, and everything which men have of themselves." (Calvin)'[40] According to Calvin we have all have nothing to do with our predestination as it is only done by the will of God. That is Calvin's opinion but I personally stand on the fact that God created each one of us with the ability to choose where we spend our eternity and God obeys the choices we make otherwise God will not go against his character or attribute of being the just God. This means that gentiles have been adopted into the family which in the time past was for the Jews as Paul affirms: Rom 11:24 (NIV) 'After all, if you were cut out of an olive tree that is wild by nature, and contrary to nature were grafted into a cultivated olive tree, how much more readily will these, the natural branches, be grafted into their own olive tree'[41] This may mean that Gentiles were made participants of the promises and inherit the blessings of God's salvation. We understand that God called Israel to be His people and that they failed to fulfil that calling.

We also understand that as the seed of Abraham, Israel was chosen by God to be a distinct people, holy to the Lord. God's purpose was for Israel to be a light to the Gentiles so that they, too, might serve God as according to (Genesis 18:17–19; Isaiah 42, 49). Rather, the Israelites pursued foreign gods and grassed their calling according

---

[40]David Guzik(2021),(enduring Word Bible Commentary Ephesians)(OnlineBible Commentary) Available: https://enduringword.com/bible-commentary/Ephesians-1/ Accessed 04/02/2021
[41] Rom 11:24(NIV)

to (Ezekiel 23; Hosea 11). Because God knew that they would do this, he already planned to restore Israel after their repentance.

Bray also draws from Calvin: 'Immediately after the greeting at the beginning of the first chapter, Paul discusses God's free election, so that the Ephesians will recognize that they have been called into the kingdom of God, because they had been chosen for [eternal] life before they were born. . . .'[42] This is a call for humility to every Christian as we are saved only by the grace of God who chose us before we were formed in our mother's womb.

Guzik draws from Clarke: 'That we should be holy and without blame before Him in love: We are chosen not only for salvation, but also for holiness. Any understanding of God's sovereign choosing that diminishes our personal responsibility for personal holiness and sanctification falls far short of the whole counsel of God. "The words [holy and without blame] are a metaphor taken from the perfect and immaculate sacrifices which the law required the people to bring to the altar of God." (Clarke)[43] This means that we are chosen to separate ourselves from sin and to dedicate our lives to the purposes of God. This means that there is the ability in every one to live a sin free life through Jesus Christ even as John articulated: John 1:8-9 'If we say that we have no sin, we deceive ourselves, and the truth is not in us. If we confess our sins, He is faithful and just to forgive us our sins, and to cleanse us from all

---

[42] Bray, Gerald L., ed. Galatians, Ephesians. Downers Grove: InterVarsity Press.2011)234
[43] David Guzik(2021),(enduring Word Bible Commentary Ephesians)(OnlineBible Commentary) Available: https://enduringword.com/bible-commentary/Ephesians-1/ Accessed 04/02/2021

unrighteousness.'[44] This means that we can live a life free from sin through repentance which is a change of behaviour and asking for forgiveness though Christ. Wright asserts: 'On the other hand, holiness was a task. That is, Israel was to live out in daily life the practical implications of their status as God's holy people.'[45] This indicates to us that holiness is a requirement for a Christian life. Although the Church is justified through Christ, the Church remains with a responsibility to live right.

In his emphasis on holiness of the Church, Wright says: 'The Church will not truly be relevant until and unless it is faithfully what it is called to be; and the identity of the Church must be defined not out of contemporary culture but out of its own story as narrated through the Scriptures, history and theology. The Church is relevant when it is being what it is with integrity. What it is called to be is the church of Jesus Christ'[46] This may explains that the church should not live recklessly but according to the expected integrity as holiness is a special attribute which marks the identity of the Church.

---

[44] John 1:8-6(KJV)
[45] Christopher H.J.Wright,*The Mission of God* (InterVarsity Press, Illinois 2006) 372
[46] Nigel G. Wright, *Free Church, Free State*(Paternoster Press, Milton Keys 2005)3

Ephesians 1:7-11

Ephesians 1:7-11(NKJV) ' In Him we have redemption through His blood, the forgiveness of sins, according to the riches of His grace, which He caused to abound toward us in all wisdom and understanding, having made known to us the mystery of His will, according to His good pleasure which He purposed in Himself, for an administration of the fullness of times, to head up all things in Christ, both the things in Heaven, and the things on earth, even in Him, in whom also we have been chosen to an inheritance, being predestined according to the purpose of Him who works all things according to the counsel of His own will,'[47] Manuel asserts: 'The idea of redemption plays a crucial role in the Sacred Scriptures. It presupposes a shipwrecked humanity, subject to misery and death, and separated from God. The words used to signify the redemptive action mean "help", "aid", "save", "assist", and express the saving actions undertaken by God, who decides to redeem humanity moved by his love, justice and holiness. Redeem is a term taken from commercial law that means "acquire again", buy, rescue, free; it was used to refer to the purchase of the life of a person or animal, a life that by sacred right belonged to God. It is said that God redeemed his people from servitude in Egypt, or that he has redeemed each individual. Any allusion to the purchase price is expressly omitted. Rescue is a concept from family law to refer to the recovery of a family's possessions. Ex 13:15; Nb 3:13 1S 14:45 Dt 9:26; 15:15; 21:8 Jr 15:21; Ho 7:13; Jb 5:20 Lv 25:25'[48] This explains the point that sin separated humanity from God and humanity became subject to

---

[47] Ephesians 1:7-11 (NKJV)
[48] Juan Manuel García de Alba | S.J. *Christ Jesus*. (Tlaquepaque: ITESO.2006)212

misery and death. There was a need of redemption which is to acquire again, to buy back or to set free. This could only be acquired through innocent blood as Paul proclaimed in Hebrews 9:22 (KJV) 'And almost all things are by the law purged with blood; and without shedding of blood is no remission.'[49] It was through his loving kindness that God provided redemption in incarnation through the atonement blood of Jesus Christ. The blood of Jesus became the purchasing price for humanity.

In the subject of redemption Manuel goes on asserting: 'In the eschatological time, God will free his people from all outside difficulties, he will gather together all those who are scattered among the other nations, and above all, he will restore them in their inner lives. Then he will free them from all their impurities and all their idols, he will heal them and redeem them from all their sins. He will give them a new heart and a new spirit. The people will walk in a single direction and down a single path. God will establish a new covenant with the House of Israel so that all may recognize him. Redemption will also have cosmic and universal dimensions; the idea of resurrection appears only in the latest writings of the Old Testament.'[50] Manuel focuses on the redemption of Israel in the eschatological future when God will restore His people back to himself according to his covenant with them through Abraham.

Silva declares: 'A metaphor used in both OT and NT to describe God's merciful and costly action on behalf of his people. The basic concept is that of release or freedom on payment of a price (but that does not mean that God paid a price to someone). In the OT the term is applied primarily

---

[49] Hebrews 9:22(KJV)
[50] Juan Manuel García de Alba | S.J. Christ Jesus. (Tlaquepaque: ITESO.2006)213

to God's deliverance of Israel from egypt through the exodus (Exod. 6:6; 15:13; Ps. 77:14 – 15; 106:9 – 11; Isa. 43:1 – 4; 51:10 – 11). But that event was only a shadow of the spiritual deliverance from sin that would be accomplished through the death of Christ (Mk. 10:45; Rom. 3:24; Eph. 1:7; 1 Pet. 1:18 – 19). Our final redemption is still in the future (Lk. 21:27 – 28; Eph. 4:30) and will take place at the resurrection (Rom. 8:23).'[51] This explains that the price of redemption was settled through the sacrificial death of Christ on the cross although another part of redemption still goes on to the eschatological future when our bodies will be redeemed from the body of sin and death as Paul illustrates: 2 Corinthians 5: 2 -4 (The Passion Translation) 'We inwardly sigh[a] as we live in these physical "tents," longing to put on a new body for our life in heaven, in the belief that once we put on our new "clothing" we won't find ourselves "naked." So, while living in this "tent," we groan under its burden, not because we want to die but because we want these new bodies. We crave for all that is mortal to be swallowed up by eternal life.'[52] This may mean that as long as we remain in this human body we remain not perfect although our spirit man yearns for perfection.

Adoption and predestination

Couenhoven declares: 'Given the ways in which doctrines of predestination have been used and abused

---

[51] redemption. (2017). In M. Silva, Essential Bible Dictionary. [Online]. Nashville: Zondervan. Available from:
https://dtl.idm.oclc.org/login?url=https://search.credoreference.com/content/entry/zonbible/redemption/0?institutionId=8909 [Accessed 6 February 2021].
[52] 2 Corinthians 5:2-4(TPT)

throughout its history, it is not hard to understand why one might have reservations about them.'[53] This explains how the doctrine of predestination is being interpreted in many different ways which may mislead us from understanding the true nature of God. These theories concerning predestination include the following: Augustine on the priority of grace, Anselm's libertarian alternative, Destiny and freedom in Aquinas, Luther and Calvin's divine determinism and finally the Barth's hopeful universalism. Of which all these can mislead if not carefully examined against the scriptures and the character of God.

Having predestined us to the adoption of children by Jesus Christ to Himself, according to the good pleasure of His will, In Him we have redemption through His blood, the forgiveness of sins, according to the riches of His grace. Guzik draws from Barclays: 'Having predestined us to adoption as sons by Jesus Christ to Himself: This is the Father's destiny for His chosen – that they would enjoy adoption as sons. God's unfolding plan for us not only includes salvation and personal transformation, but also a warm, confident relationship with the Father. In Roman law, "When the adoption was complete it was complete indeed. The person who had been adopted had all the rights of a legitimate son in his new family and completely lost all rights in his old family. In the eyes of the law he was a new person. So new was he that even all debts and obligations connected with his previous family were abolished as if they had never existed."' This proves our position as sons of God with every right as heirs of his kingdom. Guzik goes on to draw from Gaebelein: ' "Believers in the Lord Jesus Christ are not adopted into the family of God; they are born into the family. The

---

[53] Couenhoven, Jesse. *Predestination: a Guide for the Perplexed*.(London: Bloomsbury Publishing Plc.2018)2

Greek has only one word 'Sonplace.' We are placed into the position of Sons." This means that according to his own undeserved favour, God predestined all to be adopted as His own children but still God did not violet humanity's ability to choose. That is the reason we are accountable for our deeds because we exercise our right and will to choose what we want to do.

To the praise of the glory of His grace, by which He has made us accepted in the Beloved: Guzik asserts: 'The relational aspect is emphasized again as Paul describes the status of accepted (charito, "highly favored" or "full of grace" as in Luke 1:28) that is granted to every believer because of God's grace. Jesus was completely accepted by the Father. All His character, all His words, all His work was acceptable to God the Father. And now we are accepted in the Beloved.'[54] This elaborates the fact that we are fully accepted in the family of God because the atonement of his blood which Jesus made was acceptable to the father. We can approach God with boldness knowing that we have a right standing with him through our lord Jesus Christ.

God purchased our salvation which required the innocent blood as a settlement. The atonement blood of Jesus Christ became the redeeming price. God left it open to allow choice or else he would go against his own character to be the autocratic God. Lonergan affirms: 'Redemption' denotes not only an end but also a mediation, namely, the payment of price, Christ the mediator's vicarious passion and death on account of sins and for sinners , our high priest's sacrifice offered in his

---

[54] David Guzik(2021)(enduring Word Bible Commentary Ephesians)(OnlineBible Commentary) Available: https://enduringword.com/bible-commentary/Ephesians-1/ Accessed 07/02/2021

blood, his meritorious obedience, the power of the risen lord, and the intercession of the eternal priest.'[55] This explains the process of redemption that involved Jesus Christ the mediator, his atoning blood, his priesthood sacrificial death his resurrection and life of intercession. Redemption becomes an on-going process as Christ ever lives to make intercession for the Church in heaven.

Bridges comments on the grace of God: 'No one is good enough to earn salvation by himself, this definition said, so God's grace simply makes up what we lack. Some receive more grace than others; but all receive whatever they need to obtain salvation.'[56] This means that our own works cannot contribute to our salvation but only the undeserved favour of God qualifies us His salvation.

Matera elaborates: 'If we cannot be "justified" before God on the basis of what we do, then we must rely on God to justify and acquit us on the basis of his grace and favor manifested in Jesus Christ. Justification by faith means that God graciously "acquits" us, pronouncing us "innocent" because of what God has done for us in Jesus Christ rather than what we have done for God. Justification, then, is a gracious pronouncement of acquittal that only God can make. No one can "earn" such an acquittal; no one is worthy of it. But when God pronounces such an acquittal, God rectifies and justifies sinful humanity so that it stands in the correct and proper relationship to God, who is the faithful and reliable covenant God of Israel, the God and Father of Jesus Christ.'[57] This explains that in his grace God acquits,

---

[55] Bernard Lonergan: *The Redemption volume 9*, (University of Toronto Press 2018)5
[56] Bridges, Jerry. *Transforming Grace*. (Colorado Springs: NavPress Publishing Group.2017)14
[57] Matera, Frank J. *Preaching Romans : Proclaiming God's Saving*

rectifies and justifies the sinful human kind, making them to have a right standing before him the holy God not basing on human effort.

Eph 1:9-

Eph 1:9-19 NKJV) 'having made known to us the mystery of His will, according to His good pleasure which He purposed in Himself, for an administration of the fullness of times, to head up all things in Christ, both the things in Heaven, and the things on earth, even in Him, in whom also we have been chosen to an inheritance, being predestined according to the purpose of Him who works all things according to the counsel of His own will,'[58] It takes a special revelation by the Holy Spirit to understand the predestination and that God had good plans for us in his kingdom as his Children. Not everyone can understand it as it is a mystery or hidden to those without revelation of the Holy Spirit.

Eph 1:13

'in whom also you, hearing the word of truth, the gospel of our salvation, in whom also believing, you were sealed with the Holy Spirit of promise' Segovia declares: 'The stamp of a king, his 'seal', served to identify him as both the maintainer of justice and order and the source of authority; it also indirectly referred to the power of his kingdom, which sustained him in his role (Winter 1987: 61– 84). When impressed upon a letter or scroll, the mark of a seal confirmed that person's obligation to uphold or follow through on the matter it communicated. It should be noted that the author of Ephesians identifies the stamp

---

Grace. (Collegeville, MN: Liturgical Press 2010)23
[58] Eph 1:9-11 (NKJV)

of the heavenly empire as the seal of the Holy Spirit: 'After listening to the message of truth, the gospel of your salvation – having also believed, you were sealed in him with the Holy Spirit of promise' (1.13). These people are marked by God's Holy Spirit, presumably an indication that G*d has claimed them, and are given the assurance that this counter-emperor will be true to the promise of redeeming them and offering them the inheritance of the empire of God.'[59] Paul recognises the importance of the Holy Spirit as a believer's seal just as the king's stamp was highly esteemed in the Roman Empire.

Eph 1:15-17 (NKJV)

'Therefore I also, hearing of your faith in the Lord Jesus and love to all the saints, do not cease giving thanks for you, making mention of you in my prayers, that the God of our Lord Jesus Christ, the Father of glory, may give to you the spirit of wisdom and revelation in the knowledge of Him,'[60] Their faith and love for one another brought joy in Paul as this indicated the continuity of the work of God even during Paul's absence. Guzik states: 'When Paul heard of the faith and love of the Ephesians, he could do nothing else but give thanks for them. This

---

[59] Segovia, Fernando F., and Sugirtharajah, R. S., eds. *A Postcolonial Commentary on the New Testament Writings : Postcolonial Commentary on the New Testament Writings.* London: Bloomsbury Publishing 2009)269
[60] Eph 1:15-17(NKJV)

was because their faith and love were evidence of their participation in this great work of God. Faith and love do not earn us participation in this great work of God. They are evidence of our participation in God's plan. Love for all the saints: Significantly, Paul gave thanks not for their love for God, but for their love for all the saints. The real evidence of God's work in us is not the love we claim to have for Him, but our love for His people that others can see (1 John 4:20, John 13:14 and John 13:34-35).'[61] Doing the work of God is evinced in love for others as we cannot claim to love God if we cannot love those whom we can see. As their pastor Paul had a reason to rejoice and to thank God for each one of them. At times we need to make our requests known to God through thanks giving rather than asking always as Paul stated in Philippians 4:6-7

Eph 1:17-23 (KJV)

'that the God of our Lord Jesus Christ, the Father of glory, may give to you the spirit of wisdom and revelation in the knowledge of Him, the eyes of your understanding being enlightened, that you may know what is the hope of His calling, and what is the riches of the glory of His inheritance in the saints, and what is the surpassing greatness of His power toward us, the ones believing according to the working of His mighty strength which He worked in Christ in raising Him from the dead, and He seated Him at His right hand in the heavenlies, far above

---

[61]David Guzik(2021),(enduring Word Bible Commentary Ephesians)(OnlineBible Commentary) Available: https://enduringword.com/bible-commentary/Ephesians-1/ Accessed 07/02/2021

all principality and authority and power and dominion, and every name being named, not only in this world, but also in the coming age. And He has put all things under His feet and gave Him to be Head over all things to the church, which is His body, the fullness of Him who fills all in all.'[62]

Elaborating on wisdom Treier draws from the Cambridge Dictionary of Christian Theology : 'Wisdom (sophia in Greek) is an ancient theme undergoing a contemporary renaissance. As postmodernity challenges the West's modern scientism, wisdom may offer an alternative epistemology that is more holistic and less narrowly obsessed with self-evident starting points. Wisdom involves both the communication of tradition and reflective enquiry about its ongoing viability. In Scripture wisdom is the tree of life to which human beings cling so that by embracing God they may know how to live well (Prov. 3). For Augustine, whereas knowledge (scientia) relates to temporal things and human action, wisdom (sapientia) involves eternal verities – indeed, contemplation of the very divine life (Trin., 12–13).'[63] This means that Paul prayed that they may have that ability to practice what they have known about God. It is not enough knowing how to do well without the ability to put it into practice. Godly wisdom is the understanding of the ways of God as well as practising them. Worldly

---

[62] Eph 1:18-23 (NKJV)
[63] Treier, D.J. (2011). Wisdom. In I.A. McFarland, D.A.S. Fergusson, K. Kilby & et. al. (Eds.), Cambridge dictionary of Christian theology. [Online]. Cambridge: Cambridge University Press. Available from: https://dtl.idm.oclc.org/login?url=https://search.credoreference.com/content/entry/cupdct/wisdom/0?institutionId=8909 [Accessed 7 February 2021].

wisdom is different from godly wisdom as worldly wisdom can be the understanding of philosophy its scientific ways.

Paul also prays for the spirit of revelation. Silva defines revelation from Essential Bible Dictionary: 'In Christian theology, this term refers to God's disclosure of himself in nature (general revelation) and in Scripture (special revelation). The former focuses on the fact that God exists and must be honored as sovereign–a truth that is known, and has always been known, by all human beings everywhere, rendering them without excuse when they ignore him and do what is evil (Ps. 19:1 – 6 [cf. 14:1]; Rom. 1:18–20). Special revelation, on the other hand, focuses on salvation–truths about sin, grace, atonement, faith, and so on.'[64] This means that Paul was praying that God may reveal himself in a special way to the church of the Ephesians through his holy spirit. The church where God reveals himself becomes a very strong church even in times of adversity. Paul new that it depends the spiritual revelation for the church to understand the purposes of God and to participate in the victory that is given in the spiritual realm to God's children through Christ Jesus.

Ephesians 2:1-3

Ephesians 2:1-3 (NKJV) 'And He has made you alive, who were once dead in trespasses and sins in which you once walked according to the course of this world,

---

[64] revelation. (2017). In M. Silva, Essential Bible Dictionary. [Online]. Nashville: Zondervan. Available from: https://dtl.idm.oclc.org/login?url=https://search.credoreference.com/content/entry/zonbible/revelation/0?institutionId=8909 [Accessed 7 February 2021].

according to the prince of the power of the air, the spirit that now works in the children of disobedience among whom we also had our way of life in times past, in the lusts of our flesh, fulfilling the desires of the flesh and of the thoughts, and were by nature the children of wrath, even as others. But God, who is rich in mercy, for His great love with which He loved us (even when we were dead in sins) has made us alive together with Christ (by grace you are saved), so that in the ages to come He might show the exceeding riches of His grace in His kindness toward us through Christ Jesus.'[65] This is an indication that life outside Christ is spiritual death because spiritual death is the separation from God. Hughes asserts: 'What a contrast! One place is the top of the world, the other the bottom. One place is perpetually cool, the other relentlessly hot. From Mt. Whitney you look down on all of life. From Death Valley you can only look up to the rest of the world. In Ephesians 2 Paul takes us down to the Death Valley of the Soul (vv. 1–3) and then up to "the heavenly places in Christ Jesus" (vv. 4–7). His method is contrast: from death to life, from Hell to Heaven, from bondage to freedom, from pessimism to optimism. The journey's contrast will enhance our appreciation for what we have in Christ and will influence the way we live.'[66]Hughes's illustration helps us to reflect on death and life and therefore we make an informed choice having understood the implications of our choice. It is only when we are deep in the valley of death that we can actually

---

[65] Eph 2:1-7 (NKJV)
[66]From death to life. (2013). In R. Hughes, Preaching the Word: Ephesians: the mystery of the body of Christ. [Online]. Wheaton: Crossway. Available from:
https://dtl.idm.oclc.org/login?url=https://search.credoreference.com/content/entry/crossembc/from_death_to_life/0?institutionId=8909 [Accessed 7 February 2021].

acknowledge the goodness of life on the other side. At times it is after experiencing the both sides that we can actually come to an understanding of the emptiness of life outside Christ as Solomon came to a conclusion that all is vanity. Paul also considers the implications of Jesus' resurrection for our life which is the spiritual quickening.

Eph 2:8-9 (NKJV)

'For by grace you are saved through faith, and that not of yourselves, it is the gift of God, not of works, lest anyone should boast.'[67] Mcfaland draws from the Cambridge Dictionary of Christian Theology : 'Grace' is the English word normally used to translate the Greek charis in the NT and the Septuagint. The verbal cognates of charis point to its connotations of (divine) favour (Luke 1:28; cf. v. 30) and, still more specifically, gift (e.g., Rom. 8:32; 1 Cor. 2:12). In Scripture grace is associated pre-eminently with the figure of Jesus: not only did divine favour rest upon him personally (Luke 2:40, 52; John 1:14), but he is understood as the means by which that favour is transferred to others (John 1:16; Acts 15:11; Rom. 3:24; Eph. 1:7). Thus, while grace is not God's only gift to humankind, its association with Christ establishes it as that gift which completes and perfects humanity's relationship with God: 'The law was indeed given through Moses; grace and truth came through Jesus Christ' (John 1:17).'[68] This illustrates that it was due to God's divine

---

[67] Eph 2:8-9(NKJV)
[68] Mcfarland, I.A. (2011). Grace. In I.A. McFarland, D.A.S. Fergusson, K. Kilby & et. al. (Eds.), Cambridge dictionary of Christian theology. [Online]. Cambridge: Cambridge University Press. Available from: https://dtl.idm.oclc.org/login?url=https://search.credoreference.com/content/entry/cupdct/grace/0?institutionId=8909 [Accessed 7

and unmerited favour that we are saved although we did not deserve it. It is only when the Ephesian believers understood that their salvation was not because of their own effort that they would not boast against those who were still worshiping idol of Diana which might have been a very popular idol in Ephesus at that time. Guzik draws from Wood. '"Works play no part at all in securing salvation. But afterwards Christians will prove their faith by their works. Here Paul shows himself at one with James." (Wood)'[69] Although human works plays no part in salvation, there still remains a need to strive for holiness on a daily basis as Paul delaclares: Philippians 2:12 (KJV) 'Wherefore, my beloved, as ye have always obeyed, not as in my presence only, but now much more in my absence, work out your own salvation with fear and trembling.'[70] Paul is calling for purity, harmony and obedience on a daily Christian life. Osborne affirms: 'Paul clarifies that the work of developing our salvation or walk with Christ is not an isolated act on our part; it is grounded in and made possible by the greater reality that God is at work in us.'[71] This explains that even though the work of salvation was accomplished through the atonement work of Christ, we still have a task to live a life wealthy of our Christianity. Swindoll affrms: 'The Philippians are to work out their salvation not in the sense of earning it, but expressing the reality of their salvation through their practical obedience and selfless humility. The emphasis is on sanctification (learning to live more

---

February 2021].
[69]David Guzik(2021),(enduring Word Bible Commentary Ephesians)(OnlineBible Commentary) Available:
https://enduringword.com/bible-commentary/Ephesians-2/
Accessed 12/02/2021
[70] Philippians 2:12
[71]Grant Osborne, R.(Philippians Verse by Verse.) (Ashland: Lexham Press,2017)65

righteously), not on justification (being declared righteous).'[72] This elaborates the fact that we do not earn our salvation although we are accountable for our way of life as followers of Christ.

Eph 2:9 (NKJV)

'For we are His workmanship, created in Christ Jesus to good works, which God has before ordained that we should walk in them.'[73] Thayer draws from strongs: '**workmanship,** ποίημα (poiēma) Strong's Greek 4161: A thing made, a work, workmanship. From poieo; a product, i.e. Fabric.'[74] This means that we are His own master work, a work of art designed and formed by God himself for his good purposes he had for us before he formed us. Thielman asserts : 'The completely gracious nature of salvation does not mean that Paul and his readers are passive creatures but that they are new creations and should accomplish what God, their re-creator, designed them to do.'[75] This means that being God's workmanship does not make the church passive as some people take advantage of Christians just because they are religious. They begin to manipulate Christians just because they carry the name of Christianity. We still remain in the image of God with the ability to exercise our own will. Jesus was not a dupe, nor did He allow people take

---

[72] Charles Swindoll R.. (*Insights on Philippians, Colossians, Philemon.*) (Cambridge,Carol Stream: Tyndale House 2017)49

[73] Ephesians 2:10 (NKJV)

[74] Thayer's greek lexicon, Electronic Database.2002, 2003, 2006, 2011 Biblesoft, Inc. aoanline . available:www.BibleSoft.com accessed: 10/02/2021

[75] Frank Thielman. *Ephesians (Baker Exegetical Commentary on the New Testament).* Grand Rapids: Baker Academic.2010)142

advantage of Him during his ministry. Instead, He demonstrated godly servant hood maintaining certain limits. Following the guidance of the Holy Spirit, we can remain firm participating in God's work without being taken advantage of.

Eph 2:11-16 (NKJV)

'Therefore remember that you, the nations, in time past were in the flesh, who are called Uncircumcision by that which is called the Circumcision in the flesh made by hands and that at that time you were without Christ, being aliens from the commonwealth of Israel, and strangers from the covenants of promise, having no hope, and without God in the world. But now in Christ Jesus you who were once afar off are made near by the blood of Christ. For He is our peace, He making us both one, and He has broken down the middle wall of partition between us, having abolished in His flesh the enmity (the Law of commandments contained in ordinances) so that in Himself He might make the two into one new man, making peace between them and so that He might reconcile both to God in one body by the cross, having slain the enmity in Himself.'[76] This explains how the Gentiles were being discriminated by the Jews(the observers of the law) as the law considered them as it excluded them from the relationship with God and from the commonwealth of Israel which made them strangers to God's promises. It is though the atonement of the blood of Jesus Christ that we are all made to be At-One-Ment. This means that through atonement blood of Jesus both Jews and Gentiles are embraced under the same kingdom.Thieman further declares: 'By overcoming the

---

[76] Eph 2:11-12 (NKJV)

hostility between God and all human beings, Christ's death breaks down the wall of hostility between Jews and Gentiles.'[77] This explains that reconciliation between God and humanity and between Jews and the Gentiles was brought about by the atonement blood of Jesus Christ. In his postcolonial interpretation Segovia asserts: 'The suggestion of citizenship within God's domain, however it is consciously constructed, secures the idea that the household of G*d is a political entity.'[78] This indicates that in Paul's writing, the social and political environment influenced his art and science of thinking. It is very clear that there is no way we can rule out the kingdom of God from politics as the politics and kingdoms of the world generally radiant God's kingdom. Segovia goes on drawing from the works of Gombi: : 'The triumphs of Christ over the evil power vindicate the exalted status of the Lord Christ, who announces his victory by proclaiming peace. His people gather to him in unified worship as his temple, which he has founded and is building as a lasting monument to his universal sovereign lordship' (2004: 418).'[79] This may mean that the church to embrace equality and diversity may be the rejection of Christ's triumph over the kingdom of darkness. It is true that racial discrimination is still being experienced even in the Church as highlighted on *The EDI issues in the Methodist Church*: 'In 1971 the Community and Race Relations Committee came into existence and in 1978 a Notice of Motion (NOM 8) adopted by the Methodist

---

[77] Frank Thielman. Ephesians (Baker Exegetical Commentary on the New Testament).2010)148

[78] Segovia, Fernando F., and Sugirtharajah, R. S., eds. *A Postcolonial Commentary on the New Testament Writings : Postcolonial Commentary on the New Testament Writings*. 267

[79] Segovia, Fernando F., and Sugirtharajah, R. S., eds. A Postcolonial Commentary on the New Testament Writings : Postcolonial Commentary on the New Testament Writings. 268

Conference described the division between Black and White in churches in Britain as being on "the brink of heresy". It called upon the Methodist people "to turn our backs resolutely on such an understanding of Christian discipleship". Another Notice of Motion adopted by the Methodist Conference in 1978 (NOM 23) urged individual Methodist churches and church members to show openly their abhorrence of racism and fascism.'[80] This confirms that there is inequality and injustice even in the church which indicates our immaturity in the life of the kingdom of Jesus Christ and in the understanding of scriptures.

Zondervan proclaims: 'It is more precise to say that the law in its entirety has been abolished insofar as it functions as the basis of the covenant relationship between God and his people. The so-called "ceremonial" aspects were indeed a barrier separating Jews from Gentiles, but Paul is thinking in much larger terms. The old Sinai covenant rooted in Torah in its entirety has come to an end. Jesus Christ has established a new covenant that is regulated on a different basis, the presence of the Spirit.'[81] This explains that Jesus's era of grace marked the end of Moses's era of the law which promoted inequality and discrimination among God's people. Zondervan affirms further: 'The term that Paul uses here for "abolish" (καταργέω) can have the strong meaning of "destroy" (e.g., 2 Thess 2:8; 2 Tim 1:10), but in the context of a covenant or a promise, it expresses the idea of "cancelling," "voiding," or "nullifying." Paul uses this term in a handful of places in his other letters with

---

[80]Methodist Publishing, on behalf of the Methodist Church in Britain.March 2018.The EDI issues in the Methodist Church. Online. Available: https://www.methodist.org.uk/media/9017/edi-toolkit-6-final.pdf Accessed :12/-2/2021

[81] Zondervan. *Ephesians*. (Grand Rapids: HarperCollins Christian Publishing.2010)152

reference to bringing the Mosaic covenant to an end.'[82] This emphasized the fact that law does not bring division between the Jews and the Gentiles as it was removed out of the way by the blood of Jesus Christ.

Through his postcolonial view Segovia asserts: 'Clearly there is, or was, enmity between two groups within this community. Just as an emperor creates 'peace' by imposing a unity of all peoples under his reign and rule, so also the cosmic Christ, ruler over all things, is the peace between factions in the Christian community. Through Christ the two groups have become one, and they are now allowed into the presence of the king, their G*d, and have citizenship within this spiritual domain.'[83] Segovia aim to prove that Paul's writing was influenced by the contention and disunity which was between the Jews and the Gentiles as he reflects on the Roman Empire enforcing peace to those under their domain.

Eph 2:17-22 (NKJV)

'And He came and preached peace to you who were afar off, and to those who were near. For through Him we both have access by one Spirit to the Father. Now therefore you are no longer strangers and foreigners, but fellow citizens with the saints, and of the household of God, and are built upon the foundation of the apostles and prophets, Jesus Christ Himself being the chief cornerstone, in whom every building having been fitly framed together, grows into a holy sanctuary in the Lord

---

[82] Zondervan. Ephesians. (Grand Rapids: HarperCollins Christian Publishing.2010)153

[83] Segovia, Fernando F., and Sugirtharajah, R. S., eds. (*A Postcolonial Commentary on the New Testament Writings : Postcolonial Commentary on the New Testament Writings* 2009)270

in whom you also are built together for a dwelling place of God through the Spirit.'[84] This is Paul's elaboration on the unity between Jews and the Gentiles that was brought about by the atonement blood of Jesus Christ.

Eph 2:18 (KJV)

'For through Him we both have access by one Spirit to the Father.'[85] This indicates the special role of the Holy Spirit in the Godhead and in the work of reconciliation between Jews and the Gentiles and between humanity and God. This brings into question the credibility of those denominations that operates outside the Holy Spirit.

Segovia goes on with his postcolonial perspective: 'I raise these reconstruction and rebuilding components in order to shed some light on the peculiar language used to describe the ekklesia – elsewhere Paul speaks in terms of a body, not a building – and to highlight the emperor's role in construction in this general area and vested interest in the temples in particular. The rebuilding of temples for the worship of the gods and the honouring of the emperor are thus mirrored in this letter, which speaks of building the house of God for the worship of this counter-emperor.'[86] This explains how Paul uses a metaphor as he talks of God's people as new buildings of God's temple. This gives an impression that we need one another for us to make up a strong and beautiful building of God's temple. Taking the example of an African thatched hut that needs a number of poles meeting at the centre to make a roof.

---

[84] Eph 2:17-22 (NKJV)
[85] Eph 2:18 (NKJV)
[86]Segovia, Fernando F., and Sugirtharajah, R. S., eds. *A Postcolonial Commentary on the New Testament Writings : Postcolonial Commentary on the New Testament Writings.* 2009)269

No one pole can claim to be better than the other but it is their togetherness that makes them the compete roof. So as members of that makes up the building of God we need unity among us. Paul as reminds us that we are the temple of the holy spirit in 1Corinthians 6:19. Of which in my book *Equality In Diversity* I explain how the world had become a global community where people learn to live and to need one another. Embracing other races and cultures becomes a progression in civilization and racism and discrimination being the evidence of being uncivilized.

Roberts asserts: 'He still emphasizes the fundamental, initiatory, essential role of Christ in the church. But he also wants to underscore the importance of those human beings who played a founding role in the church.'[87] This indicates that Paul does not take lightly the effort of those that are called into Apostleship as himself but he clearly indicates the importance of the role of Jesus Christ as the Chief corner stone. It becomes a apostasy or cultic when we begin to celebrate the apostles giving them all the glory instead of celebrating Jesus Christ who paid the atonement price for the Church.

Eph 2:20-22(NKJV)

'in whom every building having been fitly framed together, grows into a holy sanctuary in the Lord; in whom you also are built together for a dwelling place of God through the Spirit. This may sound as if the building may initially appear to be of a different purpose but depending on the togetherness of the material used the building progress to a holy sanctuary of God. This

---

[87] Roberts, Mark D. *Ephesians*.(Grand Rapids: HarperCollins Christian Publishing.2016)84

indicates that the presence of God dwells where there is unity. We can never claim to be a church of God's presence in an organisation of racial discrimination and inequality. It is high time that as members the body of Christ we learn to come together and eliminate that barrier that identifies us as black churches or white churches.

Guzik further asserts: 'This tells us that the Church is a building, perfectly designed by the Great Architect. It is not a haphazard pile of stones, randomly dumped in a field. God arranges the Church for His own glory and purposes. This tells us that the Church is a dwelling place, a place where God lives. It is never to be an empty house that is virtually a museum, with no one living inside. The Church is to be both the living place of God and His people. This tells us that the Church is a temple, holy and set apart to God. We serve there as priests, offering the spiritual sacrifices of our lips and hearts, our praises to God (Hebrews 13:15).'[88] Guzik aims to explain that the Church is not accidentally formed but it is skilfully designed by God for his own glory and that the church are God's holy people who are united and set apart to worship and to serve God.

Eph 3:1(NKJV)

' For this cause, I, Paul, am the prisoner of Jesus Christ for you nations, if you have heard of the dispensation of the grace of God which is given to me toward you,'[89] As this book was Paul's letter from prison, Paul seeks to

---

[88]David Guzik(2021),(enduring Word Bible Commentary Ephesians)(OnlineBible Commentary) Available: https://enduringword.com/bible-commentary/Ephesians-3/ Accessed 13/02/2021
[89] Eph 3:1 (NKJV)

make the Ephesian believers to understand that his effort to bring peace between Jews and the Gentiles by bringing the gospel of salvation to the Gentiles had caused him to be in prison. Zondervan affirms: 'It is possible that some of the Gentile readers were concerned about Paul's imprisonment and thereby questioned his authority over the churches and their lives. In point of fact, Paul is in Roman custody precisely because of his unswerving and sacrificial commitment to fulfil his divine commission to make the gospel known to the Gentiles (see Acts 26:19–23). The Gentile readers of this letter are among those who owe their salvation to Paul's obedient fulfilment of his apostolic call.'[90] This elaborates the fact that it was not Jesus that put Paul in prison although Paul might be misinterpreted for being a prisoner of God but that he was in prison God's purpose of extending the gospel of the grace of God to the Gentiles.

Eph 3:3-7(NKJV)

' that by revelation He made known to me the mystery (as I wrote before in few words by which, when you read, you may understand my knowledge in the mystery of Christ)which in other ages was not made known to the sons of men, as it is now revealed to His holy apostles and prophets by the Spirit that the nations should be fellow heirs, and of the same body, and partaker of His promise in Christ through the gospel. Of this gospel I was made a minister, according to the gift of the grace of God given to me by the effectual working of His power.[91] This means

---

[90] Zondervan.(*Ephesians*..2010)176
[91] Eph 3:3-7(KJV)

that the gospel of the grace of God towards the Gentiles was only revealed to Paul as some apostles like Peter still had a problem with the gentiles for not observing the Jewish laws in Galatians 2:11-14. Keener asserts: 'Yet now Peter, who knew that there was nothing inherently wrong with this gentile sort of lifestyle, was compelling gentiles to adopt a Jewish lifestyle. This compulsion violated the agreement that allowed both groups to follow their own culture (2:9; Acts 15:29; 21:21, 25), an agreement that Paul believed he still followed. 742'[92] This indicates the discrimination which was in Peter's attitude as he was trying to enforce the Jewish culture to the gentiles. This makes me to reflect on the how the gospel was taken to Africa from the west and how they disregarded the African culture and traditions of approaching God to promote their own ways which they considered to be godlier and the African ways of worship as demonic. This approach caused many Africans to reject Jesus Christ as they associated him with their white colonisers.

Eph 3:8-9 (NKJV)

'This grace is given to me (who am less than the least of all saints) to preach the gospel of the unsearchable riches of Christ among the nations and to bring to light what is the fellowship of the mystery which from eternity has been hidden in God, who created all things by Jesus Christ;'[93] Just because Paul was the last to be called into apostleship ,he considers himself to be less than the least of all saints. Osborne declares: 'Grace (Charis) in Ephesians is always connected to Paul's gift of salvation

---

[92] Keener, Craig S. *Galatians : A Commentary*. (Grand Rapids: Baker Academic.2019)174
[93] Eph 3:8-9(NKJV)

by the blood of Christ. The extension of God's salvation to all the peoples of the earth is entirely the result of God's grace and mercy, as is the gift of life to undeserving sinners. Moreover, God gave this grace-gift to Paul, to become "apostle to the Gentiles" and to be used by God to bring many into the kingdom.'[94] Paul use the word grace to illustrate how the Gentiles were undeserving the salvation which was before considered as belonging to the Jews (The chosen generation)

Eph 3:10-11 (NKJV)

'so that now to the rulers and powers in the heavenlies might be known by the church the manifold wisdom of God according to the eternal purpose which He purposed in Christ Jesus our Lord in whom we have boldness and access with confidence through His faith.'[95] Osborne further asserts: 'The church through its triumphant mission makes known God's wisdom to the cosmic powers, and the unfolding wisdom of God is completely in accordance with his eternal purpose in creating this world and producing his salvation in it. The term for "purpose" (prothesis) is the same as in 1:11, where it was used of the divine plan that is the basis of our predestination. This could be translated as God's "planned purpose" that lay behind the coming of Christ, as well as the salvation that has resulted from it. That purpose is eternal; every part of God's plan— from creation to the new creation in Christ to the final creation of the new heavens and new earth— is encompassed in it.'[96] This means that the church is the manifestation of the victory that came through the

---

[94] Osborne, Grant R. *Ephesians Verse by Verse*. (Oak Harbor: Lexham Press.2017)
[95] Osborne, Grant R. *Ephesians Verse by Verse*. 64
[96] Osborne, Grant R. Ephesians Verse by Verse. 64

atonement death of Jesus Christ even as Paul in Colossians 2:15 (AMP) 'God disarmed the principalities and powers that were ranged against us and made a bold display and public example of them, in triumphing over them in Him and in it [the cross].'[97] This means that triumph over the devil was pre-planned by God to be displayed publicly. Therefore there is no need of being ashamed to declare the gospel of Jesus Christ in public as Jesus demonstrated victory publicly on the cross.

Eph 3:12(NKJV)

'in whom we have boldness and access with confidence through His faith.'[98] Guzik declares: 'The fact of this unity is shown by the truth that we (Jew and Gentile collectively) have the identical boldness, access, and confidence before God – because it has nothing to do with national or ethnic identity, only with faith in Him (Jesus).'[99] This is an indication of the power of faith in Jesus Christ as it breaks through all barriers of racial discrimination. I believe that there is nothing on earth that unifies people than their faith in Christ. It is in church where we see people of different races working and fellowshipping together and even getting into marriage covenants.

Guzik goes on to draw from Gaebelein ' The word for boldness has the idea of "freedom of speech." We have the freedom to express ourselves before God, without fear or shame. "The Greek word 'parresia' translated by

---

[97] Col 2:15 (AMP)
[98] Eph 3:12(KJV)
[99] David Guzik(2021),(enduring Word Bible Commentary Ephesians)(OnlineBible Commentary) Available: https://enduringword.com/bible-commentary/Ephesians-3/ Accessed 13/02/2021

'boldness' means really 'free speech' – that is, the speaking of all. It is the blessed privilege of prayer.'"[100] This indicates the boldness that faith in Christ embraces. I believe that this boldness does not only come through faith in Christ alone but through prayer and the holy Spirit that is given to those who have faith in Jesus Christ as Luke reflected in Acts 4:31(AMP) 'And when they had prayed, the place where they were meeting together was shaken [a sign of God's presence]; and they were all filled with the Holy Spirit and began to speak the word of God with boldness and courage.'[101] This evidences the fact that faith in Christ, prayer and the Holy Spirit gives boldness to preach the truth of gospel publicly. It is a shame that at this post-modernity era many preachers of the gospel compromise the meaning and the power of scripture by trying to maintain political correctness rather than telling the whole truth from the scriptures with the example of some sensitive topics like that of homosexuality. It is this boldness that caused Peter's public proclamation: 'Acts 5:29(The Passion Translation) 'Peter and the apostles replied, "We must listen to and obey God more than pleasing religious leaders.'[102] The apostles chose to risk their lives rather than compromising in order to maintain their political correctness.

---

[100]David Guzik(2021),(enduring Word Bible Commentary Ephesians)(OnlineBible Commentary) Available: https://enduringword.com/bible-commentary/Ephesians-3/ Accessed 13/02/2021
[101] Acts 4:31 (AMP)
[102] Acts 5:29 (TPT)

Eph 3:13 (NKJV)

'For this reason I desire that you faint not at my tribulations for you, which is your glory'[103] Paul seeks to make himself an example of boldness even as it resulted to his incarceration.

Eph 3:14-17 (NKJV)

'For this cause I bow my knees to the Father of our Lord Jesus Christ of whom the whole family in Heaven and earth is named that He would grant you, according to the riches of His glory,to be strengthened with might by His Spirit in the inner man; that Christ may dwell in your hearts by faith; that you, being rooted and grounded in love'[104] Osborne proclaims: 'Paul's own suffering prompts him to think of what the Christians in the province of Asia are going through for Christ. There was indeed intense persecution, as seen in 1 Peter and, reflecting the situation thirty years later, in Revelation; both these letters were written to churches in the area. Paul's point throughout this section is that his and their suffering is more than worthwhile, since through them the gospel is being proclaimed and the mystery of Christ being worked out in the growth of the church. All of this takes place in the midst of, and partly because of, all they are going through. Paul has never minded afflictions as long as they are serving the cause of Christ (see Rom 8:31– 39; 1 Cor 12:21– 29).'[105] Paul seeks to let the believers of Ephesus know that he was interceding for them to be as bold as himself in times of adversity as they also the church was facing opposition and persecution

---

[103] Eph 3:13(NKJV)
[104] Eph 3:14-17(NKJV)
[105] Osborne, Grant R. Ephesians Verse by Verse. 65

from the Roman Empire and he wants them never to be discouraged even by his own suffering.

Cohick asserts: 'Paul describes his posture— kneeling— rather than stating directly that he is praying. This vivid word picture has Old Testament resonances for Paul. In Rom 14:11 and Phil 2:10, Paul draws on Isa 45:23 in his convictions that every knee will bow to honor Christ and God the Father (see also Rom 11:4, citing 1 Kgs 19:18). Some suggest that the hymn in Phil 2:5– 11 was well known to Paul's churches. If the Ephesians were also aware of it, Paul's posture before God would call to mind the promised victory of Christ. Paul presents a picture of humility, but also one of tremendous hope, for his bowed knee foreshadows the eschatological event where all render appropriate obeisance to God. It is unclear whether earliest Christians often knelt in prayer, but perhaps the physical act of kneeling today would be a useful reminder to believers of the eschatological event in which God's majesty will be honored by all.'[106] This illustrates the need for humility in the presence of God. They are many forms of prayer which include prayer walk or lying prostrate in the presence of the lord but kneeling portrays total submission and concentration before the lord. It is a shame that we live in a generation of people who are too busy with smart phones text messages, chatting and internet browsing while they are in prayer. Kneeling may carry a lot of meanings like a sign of respect and deference. In the pas people kneeled before queens, kings and altars. Nowadays one can kneel to kneel to beg or even to ask someone to marry them. One can also kneel to get down the level of a child. Kneeling can also be a position of sadness and bereavement. Recently footballers adopted

---

[106]Cohick, Lynn H.. 2010. Ephesians. Eugene: Wipf and Stock Publishers.2010)94

the kneeling of one knee as a sign a protest against violence and brutality of the USA police against black people. Paul is painting a picture of humility and submission as he prays for the church of Ephesus.

Thielman affirms: 'This is one of the few times that Paul describes his posture in prayer. Kneeling was a symbol of deep respect for the person addressed. The man with leprosy paid Jesus this respect when he knelt before him and asked for healing. Paul knelt on the beach and prayed with the leaders of the Ephesian church the last time he saw them. When Jesus prayed he often stood and looked into the sky (see Mark 7:34; John 17:1).'[107] This shows that there is no one specific body posture that may make our prayers more acceptable, only the condition of the heart is what God is much concerned with as one can physically kneel yet they remain proud and absolutely pompous in their attitude of the heart.

Eph 3:18-19 (NKJV)

'may be able to comprehend with all saints what is the breadth and length and depth and height and to know the love of Christ which passes knowledge, that you might be filled with all the fullness of God.'[108] Paul indicates his reason for his prayer that Ephesian believers may have the understanding and the revelation of the love of God. It is this understanding and the revelation of the love of God towards them that would keep them determined even to death knowing that God is pleased with them and that God has not left them to go through tribulation alone. Roberts

---

[107] Thielman, Frank S., Baugh, Steven M., and Arnold, Clinton E. *Ephesians, Philippians, Colossians, Philemon*. Grand Rapids: HarperCollins Christian Publishing.2015)61
[108] Eph 3:18-19 (NKJV)

declares: 'This passage encourages us to seek a deeper knowledge and experience of God's power, love, and presence. It opens our eyes to the untapped potential of God's power in us, inspiring us to live for the praise of God's glory in new and bold ways.'[109] This means that prayer can lead us to the new adventures in God's presence and a better way of understanding the love of God. Prayer does not change God but it changes and transforms those that pray. Prayer stimulates and ignites the power or potential that is dormant and undeveloped within us.

Eph 3:20-21(NKJV)

'Now to Him who is able to do exceeding abundantly above all that we ask or think, according to the power that works in us to Him be glory in the church by Christ Jesus throughout all ages, forever. Amen.'[110] It is after we have existed all our plans and ideas that God begins to manifest his own power. It looks like Paul had existed his own ideology that he finally submit to God's will with the understanding that God has got that ability or dexterity which is not found in humans. I define the word able which Paul uses from the American Heritage Dictionary : 'from The American Heritage(R) Dictionary of the English Language: 'Having sufficient power or resources to accomplish something'[111] This means that Paul came to

---

[109] Roberts, Mark D. *Ephesians*. (Grand Rapids: HarperCollins Christian Publishing.2016)104
[110] Eph 3:20-21(NKJV)
[111] Able. (2016). In Editors of the American Heritage Dictionaries (Ed.), The American Heritage (R) dictionary of the English language. (6th ed.). [Online]. Boston: Houghton Mifflin. Available from: https://dtl.idm.oclc.org/login?url=https://search.credoreference.com/content/entry/hmdictenglang/able/0?institutionId=8909 [Accessed 13 February 2021].

an understanding and a revelation that only God has that sufficient power or resources to accomplish that which the Church of Ephesus real needed.

Eph 4:1-2(NKJV)

'I therefore, the prisoner in the Lord, beseech you that you walk worthy of the calling with which you are called with all lowliness and meekness, with long-suffering, forbearing one another in love.'[112] Bray draws from Erasmus 'Sincere preachers exhort and implore their churches; they do not issue commands, try to control their consciences or bully them. Paul's words here are those of a sincere preacher. To walk worthy of the calling to which we have been called is to demonstrate that our calling comes from God by producing as many fruits worthy of it as we can, by being content with our position, with our gifts, by not being jealous of others because of their callings or gifts, not to try to copy the callings and gifts of others, to embellish the Sparta that we have found and make it fruitful by the use of our gifts. To walk worthy of our calling is the general way by which unity of doctrine, peace and harmony will prevail in the church, because it is the prerequisite for the other gifts to flourish.'[113] This is a calling to live a life worthy of Christianity standards.

This is a great lesson from Erasmus as he reflected on the personality of Paul that is displayed in his humble words. Erasmus reminds preachers of the gospel to maintain humility in their presentation of the gospel and not use their position of authority to bully or dominate the church of God. We should always remember as servants

---

[112] Eph 4:1-3(NKJV)
[113] Bray, Gerald L., ed. *Galatians, Ephesians*. (Downers Grove: InterVarsity Press.2011)327

of God that we are called to serve the people and not to be masters. In the Old Testament God was not pleased with the leaders of Israel who mistreated and manipulated the flock. Ezekiel 34:2-5

Bruce asserts: ' Because the basic facts of our holy faith are such as have been set forth, Christians ought to live in accordance with them; their character and conduct should match their creed and confession. In this epistle, where Christians are taught the hope of their calling (Ephesians 1:18), Paul insists that their earthly behavior should be worthy of that calling.'[114]

I personally do not agree with Erasmus that working worthy of our calling is producing a s many fruits as we can because Paul was not referring to winning people to Christ in this sense but Paul was literally encouraging Christians in Ephesus to walk in the lowliness and meekness of the heart being patient with one another in unity and love. In general Paul mentions Humility, Gentleness and Patience.

Osborne affirms: '(1) Humility and gentleness. There is no place among Christ's followers for pride. Christ exemplified servant leadership, demanding the same of his followers (Mark 9:35; 10:41– 45). Paul emphasizes the importance of this calling by stating that the Ephesians should live with " all humility and gentleness," making this a supreme mandate and connecting the two words into a single idea. This went against Greco-Roman practices of the day, which exemplified the belief that "meekness is

---

[114] Chapter 4. (2012). In F. Bruce, *The epistle to the ephesians*. [Online]. Nashville: Kingsley Books, Inc. Available from: https://dtl.idm.oclc.org/login?url=https://search.credoreference.com/content/entry/ccltdepistle/chapter_4/0?institutionId=8909 [Accessed 19 February 2021].

weakness" and that the highest qualities are proven by self-serving success (much as in "the American way"). Jesus completely reversed this pagan practice, making humility one of the most important of the virtues in the eyes of God. To be honest, I have witnessed a lack of humility in all too many Christian leaders. We must come to realize that pride is one of the truly deadly sins in the eyes of God; it is only when we acknowledge this that we can be honest with ourselves regarding the true level of our humility.'[115] This emphasizes the fact that Christians should walk in humility as pride has no place in the kingdom of God. Osborne also elaborates that being humble is not a sign of weakness as it was considered in the Greco-Roman ways of life. On the same note Osborne further asserts: 'The Bible regularly castigates arrogance and self-centeredness. Perhaps the clearest expression of this is Philippians 2:3– 4: "Do nothing out of selfish ambition or vain conceit. Rather, in humility value others above yourselves, not looking to your own interests but each of you to the interests of the others." Humility demands a life directed toward others rather than toward self-aggrandizement.'[116] This indicates that arrogance and self-centredness which comes through pride should not be part of a Christian life.

Elaborating on the Paul's second point of Humility, Osborne further asserts: 'The other word Paul uses, "gentleness," way in which a life of humility treats others: with kindness and concern. This quality too highly prized in Scripture. The Greek word (*prautes*) here is often translated "humble" or even "the poor" (who had to throw themselves under God's care). And gentleness, a "fruit of

---

[115] Osborne, Grant R.*Ephesians Verse by Verse*. (Oak Harbor: Lexham Press.2017)76
[116] Osborne, Grant R.*Ephesians Verse by Verse*. 76,77

the Spirit" (Gal 5:22– 23), is certainly a prime attitude we need to adopt when admonishing another person (Gal 6:1; 2 Tim 2:25). .'[117] This means Christians should treat others with kindness. In actual fact kindness should automatically be part of the Christian life as it is birthed by the presence of the Holy Spirit who is the seal Christians.

White draws from Calvin: 'For John Calvin, humility alone exalts God as sovereign; it is part of self-denial, the abandonment of self-confidence that constitutes faith. (Calvin insisted on being buried in an unmarked grave.) Puritans cultivated humility as an antidote to self-righteousness, by constant self-examination. Jonathan Edwards thought humility an essential test of religious emotionalism.'[118] This means that when we humble ourselves we actually acknowledge God's position of supremacy. Kelvin decided to be buried in an unmarked grave probably because he wanted to avoid the temptation of being idolised as great man of God who ever lived. In humility we learn to step back even in family arguments and let the other to win in that argument.

Osborne elaborates on Patience: 'Patience. The Greek term (makrothymia) literally means "a long time before one gets angry." Connoting a person with a long fuse, it is often translated "long-suffering" and describes the manner in which God puts up with sinful humanity. Indeed, he is described as being "slow to anger" (Exod 34:6; Neh 9:17;

---

[117]Osborne, Grant R.*Ephesians Verse by Verse*. 77
[118] White, R.E. (2017). Humility. In W.A. Elwell, Evangelical dictionary of theology. (3rd ed.). [Online]. Ada: Baker Publishing Group. Available from: https://dtl.idm.oclc.org/login?url=https://search.credoreference.com/content/entry/bpgugxt/humility/0?institutionId=8909 [Accessed 14 February 2021].

Ps 145:8; Joel 2:13; Jas 1:19) and "patient" (Rom 2:4; 2 Pet 3:9). In the New Testament the need for patience in church relationships is frequently discussed as a key virtue (2 Cor 6:6; Col 3:12). Paul tells the Thessalonians to "be patient with everyone" (1 Thess 5:14) and defines this quality as a core aspect of love (1 Cor 13:4).'[119] This may be calling for Christians to give others another chance and never to right anyone off because of their first mistake bearing in mind that humans are not infallible but they are subject to mistakes. I personally began to train myself to call the other person what I want them to become.

Collins draws from Taylor: 'It is very strange ... that the years teach us patience; that the shorter our time, the greater our capacity for waiting. Taylor, Elizabeth A Wreath of Roses (1950).'[120] This indicates that patience is a sign of maturity which may develop with age.This is true of my own life ,of which during my early years as a young man I did not have the capacity to wait or to give someone else a second chance but as I grow a bit older I find myself able to look aside on certain mistakes people do knowing that no one is perfect except God.

Paul also mentioned bearing with one another in love. Osborne further affirms: 'Bearing with one another in love. In one sense this further defines patience, describing how patience works itself out in our social interactions within the church. In another sense it defines how we are to "walk worthily" before God by extending and combining all of the attributes discussed thus far and

---

[119] Osborne, Grant R.*Ephesians Verse by Verse*. 77
[120] Patience. (2003). In Collins dictionary of quotations. (2nd ed.). [Online]. London: Collins. Available from: https://dtl.idm.oclc.org/login?url=https://search.credoreference.com/content/entry/hcdquot/patience/0?institutionId=8909 [Accessed 14 February 2021].

thereby becoming a separate category. God's people exercise humility, gentleness, and patience by putting up with each other. The concept is related to endurance—specifically to how we are to tolerate each other's foibles and peccadilloes. For instance, Jesus, in his frustration at the disciples' inability to cast out a demon, exclaimed, "How long shall I put up with you?" (Mark 9:19). And Barnabas in Acts 15:37– 39 not only put up with Mark's (likely) youthful rebellion but split up with Paul in order to take Mark back home to Cyprus and disciple him so that he might become the great Christian leader he would later prove to be.'[121] This summons us to learn from Paul's teachings to the Ephesians as followers of Christ we to bear with each other's weaknesses with the understanding that they will become better with time. I learn to give someone else the benefit of doubt. I leant to treat someone else the way I want them to become.

Eph 4:3-6 (NKJV)

'endeavoring to keep the unity of the Spirit in the bond of peace There is one body and one Spirit, even as you are called in one hope of your calling, one Lord, one faith, one baptism one God and Father of all, who is above all and through all and in you all.'[122] Paul is encouraging the believers to maintain unity and peace as there is a high risk of divisions among them because of persecutions which the church was going through from the Roman Empire. Paul is using a human body as typology of the Church. The entire human body is work together in unity so it is with a healthy Church.

---

[121] Osborne, Grant R. *Ephesians Verse by Verse.* 77
[122] Eph 4:3-6

Bruce elucidates: *'endevouring to keep the unity of the Spirit in the bond of peace.*

The unity spoken of here is the unity of heart which the Spirit of God fosters in a community of believers. The English word "unity" (and the underlying Greek word henotes) can have more than one meaning, and we should not interpret "unity" here by relating it to the recurring "one" of verses 4-6. In verses 4-6 it is uniqueness that is intended. The unity of the Spirit here is a different thing from the statement that there is "one Spirit" in verse 4. The fact that there is one Spirit of God is something which cannot be affected by any endeavor or action of men one way or the other. But in the present passage Paul is inculcating the same mutual attitude as when in Philippians 2:2 he exhorts the Philippian Christians to "be of the same mind, having the same love, being of one accord, of one mind." If that is so, then "the unity of the Spirit" is best maintained when Christians have this mind in them "which was also in Christ Jesus" (Philippians 2:5). Or, to put it otherwise, when the graces commended in verse 2 are cultivated, the unity of the Spirit is preserved. The expression here bears practically the same meaning as "the communion of the Holy Spirit" in 2 Corinthians 13:14. And those in whom the unity of the Spirit is displayed will be joined together "in the bond of peace." We may compare Colossians 3:14, where love is the perfect "bond" (Gk. *syndesmos*, as here) which binds the other Christian graces together. God is the author of peace, and the sowing of "discord among brethren" (the opposite of keeping the unity of the Spirit) is an abomination in his sight (cf. Proverbs 6:16,19b). This indicates that it is the mind of Christ, love for each other and the Holy Spirit who fosters this kind of unity among believers.

Tenney asserts: 'Paul took special interest in the unity within the body of believers, and he did not argue for an invisible bond but for a oneness that should characterize the visible body. He recognized unity in diversity and diversity in unity, and he amplified this approach (1 Cor. 12) with the appeal to love as the unifying bond (ch. 13). The apostle looked upon unity as reality already in existence, but also as a reality yet to be attained. As we are "patient, bearing with one another in love," we are then eager "to keep the unity of the Spirit" (Eph. 4:2-3).'[123] This explains how Paul understood the power of unity in the Church. This indicates how diversified were the Churches of Paul. Paul did not only speak of unity in theory but the practical unity that could be experienced in the church. It is easy to talk or teach things which are not practical in real life but Paul was not such a preacher who was interested in well-articulated sermons that are only theoretical. This is the reason Paul proclaims in 1 Cor 2:4 (AMPC) 'And my language and my message were not set forth in persuasive (enticing and plausible) words of wisdom, but they were in demonstration of the [Holy] Spirit and power [a proof by the Spirit and power of God, operating on me and stirring in the minds of my hearers the most holy emotions and thus persuading them],'[124] This explains that Paul was not interested in empty and enticing words but he real wanted to see the evidence of unity in the body of Christ. The scripture also tells us that God commands a blessing where there is unity in Psalms 133:1-3

Eph 4:7-12 (NKJV)

---

[123] Tenney, Merrill C., and Douglas, J. D. Zondervan Illustrated Bible Dictionary. Grand Rapids: HarperCollins Christian Publishing.2011)1497
[124] 1 Cor 2:4(AMPC)

'But to every one of us is given grace according to the measure of the gift of Christ. Therefore He says, "When He ascended up on high, He led captivity captive and gave gifts to men." (Now that He ascended, what is it but that He also descended first into the lower parts of the earth? He who descended is the same also as He who ascended up far above all heavens, that He might fill all things.)And truly He gave some to be apostles, and some to be prophets, and some to be evangelists, and some to be pastors and teachers for the perfecting of the saints, for the work of the ministry, for the edifying of the body of Christ. Paul wanted it to be clear that everyone in the body of Christ is given the favour even if they do not deserve it. It is this favour or grace that helps us to meet and to overcome challenges of life as individuals.

Osborne proclaims: 'An important truth implicit in verse 7 is that God does not give gifts on the basis of race or social status. They are distributed equally to "each one of us," and the basis is "as Christ apportioned it" (literally, "the measure of the gift of Christ"). In other words diversity is grounded in unity, for the entire body is involved. In 1 Corinthians 12:11 it is the Spirit "who distributes them to each one, just as he determines," while here it is Christ who is in sovereign control of the gifts. Paul describes them as grace-gifts; the very term for spiritual gift is (Rom 12:6; 1 Cor 12:4), meaning "grace given" to a person. Charisma'[125] It is important to know that God never discriminate any one when it comes to gifts but he gives all of us the gifts and talents according to his for knowledge. It also means that God does not give talents for personal gain or pride but for us to complement and qualify each other as members of the same body. It is this understanding that stops each one of us from pride

---

[125] Osborne, Grant R. *Ephesians Verse by Verse*. (2017)82

and boasting knowing that whatever the talent we have it is for the benefit of the Church of Jesus Christ.

Osborne further affirms: 'The emphasis here is on the source of these graces: Christ. There is no haphazard, random distribution of gifts. Every gift is carefully chosen and apportioned according to the sovereign will of God. In our narcissistic world we too often are dissatisfied with what Christ has given us and want more. That is to deny God's grace and will for the sake of self. God gives us exactly what he wants us to have and what is best for us. It is our privilege to unquestioningly accept and use his gracious gifts. The joint ministry we have in the church is the result of the particular gifts each of us has received.'[126] This means that God carefully choose those to give a particular talent. It is the understanding that God gives us what is best for the entire church that makes us to celebrate each other rather than trying to compete or becoming jealousy of each other.

Commenting on Paul's proclamation Osborne further asserts: 'Paul now provides commentary on the meaning of Christ "ascending on high" in the psalm quote, looking at the chronology of events that led to Christ's exaltation. He begins with "What does 'he ascended' mean except that he also descended to the lower, earthly regions?" (NIV). The last part of the verse literally reads, "descended into the lower parts of the earth." This has led to a number of interpretations: descensus ad inferos (1) The lower parts are the underworld, and this describes , or Jesus' "descent into Hades" at his death. This is paralleled by similar interpretations of Romans 10:6– 7 ("descend into the deep") and 1 Peter 3:19 (Christ preaching to the spirits in prison) and has long been a popular view; it goes

---

[126] Osborne, Grant R. Ephesians Verse by Verse. (2017)82

back to Tertullian and Jerome and is found in the Apostles' Creed. This view is indeed viable, for these Gentile Christians would have grown up with stories about the underworld. If we understand Hades to be the grave, it would refer in a poignant way to Christ's death. Yet it seems to be a strange way to speak of the death and burial of Jesus.'[127] Connecting Paul's ideology with a parable in Luke 16:19-31 and Romans 10:6-7 this highlights a school of thought by Tertullian and Jerome about Jesus descending to hell to preach to the dead and to relocate paradise which might have been located just above hell where the rich man in hell could see Lazarus from Paradise. There is an idea that Jesus went to recover all the powers that the devil had gained at the fall of Adam. The ideology goes on to proclaim that when Jesus finally declared a great commission to his disciples claiming that 'all power is given unto me in heaven and on earth' Matthew 28:18-19

Paul speaks of five categories of office given by Jesus before his ascension which are apostles, prophets, evangelists, pastors, and teachers. Foulkes elaborates: 'First stood the apostles. First in time and first in importance, Masson puts it. The word apostolos is used in three different ways in the New Testament. It could mean simply a messenger, as is the case apparently in Philippians 2:25 we can neglect that meaning here. It was used above all for the twelve, who in many parts of the New Testament are given a special and distinctive position 1 Cor 15:5'[128] According to Foulkes Apostleship is the first most important calling. What makes them most important is that Apostles marked the foundation of the Church just as in building upon the foundation stands the

---

[127] Osborne, Grant R. Ephesians Verse by Verse. (2017)82
[128] Foulkes, Francis. *Ephesians*. Illinois: (InterVarsity Press.2008)124

whole building. No matter how beautiful or high the building can be its strength is determined by the strength of its foundation.

Gordon asserts : 'The biblical apostles were the leaders of the first generation of the Christian movement. In more recent times, various Protestant and other religious leaders have claimed the title as well. The exalted status of the original apostles in the geographically expanding church was based on having known and followed Jesus prior to his crucifixion and resurrection. Paul claimed apostolic status based on his encounter with Jesus on the road to Damascus (Acts 9; I Corinthians 15:8-10). Through the centuries, the church claimed that authority had been passed to it from the original 12 apostles (minus Judas and plus Matthias) and Paul. The Apostles' Creed was seen as a summary of what the apostles taught. The apostles had passed authority to the bishops through the laying on of hands during their consecration service. The bishops in turn passed authority to congregational leaders through their ordaining the priests. Reformation-era churches held differing views on apostolic authority. The Anglican and some Lutheran churches continued to claim apostolic succession for their episcopacy.'[129] This is an indication that this office of apostles continues to this day as various Protestants, Pentecostals and Charismatics leaders continue to claim the title of an apostle. It as though it is no longer based on the having followed Jesus prior to his crucifixion as Jesus continues to reveal himself to certain individuals even to this day as he revealed himself to Paul

---

[129] Gordon, M.J. (2016). apostles. In J.G. Melton, Encyclopedia of world religions: Encyclopedia of Protestantism. (2nd ed.). [Online]. New York: Facts On File. Available from: https://dtl.idm.oclc.org/login?url=https://search.credoreference.com/content/entry/fofecvt/apostles/0?institutionId=8909 [Accessed 17 February 2021].

on his way to Damascus. It may be questionable that Catholics claim to receive Apostleship through succession by laying of hands by the Pope whom they believe he received his apostleship from Peter.

Foulkes draws from Barclay: 'Next come the evangelists. Only two other references to these in the New Testament can guide us as to their function and work. In Acts 21:8 Philip, whose four daughters were prophets, is called an evangelist, and in 2 Timothy 4:5 Timothy is told to 'do the work of an evangelist'. We may assume that theirs was an itinerant work of preaching under the apostles, and it may be fair to call them 'the rank and file missionaries of the church' (Barclay).'[130] What makes the Evangelists second most important is that they bring people who make up the kingdom just as it is in the literal building after the foundation is laid there is a need for the building material for the walls to start going up. Evangelist brings the building material which are the souls or people drawn into the kingdom.

Foulkes further declares: 'Then, linked together (by the same article in the Gk.) are the pastors and teachers . It is possible that this phrase describes the ministers of the local church, whereas the first three categories are regarded as belonging to the universal church. More likely, the dominant thought is still of spiritual functions and gifts. Apostles and evangelists had a special task in planting the church in every place, prophets for bringing a particular word from God to a situation. Pastors and teachers were gifted to be responsible for the day-to-day building up of the church. There is no hard and fast line to be drawn between the two. The duties of the pastor (literally 'shepherd') are to feed the flock with spiritual

---

[130] Foulkes, Francis. *Ephesians* 2008)125

food and to see that they are protected from spiritual danger. Our Lord used the word in John 10 :11 , 14 to describe his own work, and he continues to be the chief pastor (Heb. 13:20 ; 1Pet. 5:2 ;5:4) under whom others are called to 'Tend the flock of God' (1 Pet. 5: 2 ; cf. John 21 :15-17 ; Acts 20:28). Every pastor must be 'an apt teacher' (1Tim. 3:2 ; cf. Titus 1:9), though it is evident that some have pre-eminently the gift of teaching, and may be said to form a particular division of ministry within the church, and to be a special gift of Christ to his people (Acts 13:1 ; Rom.12:7 ; 1 Cor. 12:28.'[131] This indicates that teachers and pastors have the same value of looking after the church. It is the strong and sound teaching that keep the church from other doctrines of the enemy which are meant to mislead. It may be a requirement for the pastor to have the ability to teach which is a way of feeding the flock of God or building up the kingdom as illustrated by The prophet: Jeremiah 3:15 (NIV) 'Then I will give you shepherds after my own heart, who will lead you with knowledge and understanding'[132] This means that God is very much concerned about the pastors who have the ability to teach. Gone are the days when people would only rely on the revelation of the Holy Spirit neglecting to study and prepare for the church service as Paul declares: 2 Timothy 2:15 (AMPC) ' Study and be eager and do your utmost to present yourself to God approved (tested by trial), a workman who has no cause to be ashamed, correctly analysing and accurately dividing [rightly handling and skilfully teaching] the Word of Truth.'[133] This indicates that without knowledge the pastors may make fools of themselves in front of the church especially in this digital generation that is exposed

---

[131] Foulkes, Francis. *Ephesians* 2008)126
[132] Jere 3:15(NIV)
[133] 2 Tim 2:15(AMPC)

to a lot free information and the online preaching. With the lock down and gathering being forbidden most people are now doing church online with different preachers of different teaching skills and abilities.

Paul also mentioned the office of Prophets after the Apostles. Unlike Foukes I wouldn't think that prophets are the least important among all other offices. Rather I would classify prophets on the second position as Paul did because most important was the voice and the guidance from the lord Jesus on how to build the church of which he would communicate through prophecy.

Wigoder draws from the New Encyclopedia of Judaism: 'The prophets were charismatic figures, believed to be endowed with the Divine gift of receiving and imparting messages revealed to them by God. Prophecy is the delivery of these messages, not the ability to look into the future. The prophet was the intermediary between the Divine Will and the people. The concept was known to other peoples in the Ancient Near East, so the ancient Israelites took seriously, for example, Balaam, the prophet-soothsayer sent by the king of Moab to curse them (Num. 22). The first person to be called a prophet in the Bible was Abraham (Gen. 21:7), while Moses was regarded as the greatest of the prophets (Deut. 34:10), a belief formulated by Maimonides in his Principles of Faith'[134]. This means that Prophets had important role in the body of Christ as they were the seers and the mouth piece of God. The anointing in their lives allowed them to

---

[134] Prophets and prophecy. (2002). In G. Wigoder, F. Skolnik & S. Himelstein (Eds.), The new encyclopedia of Judaism. (2nd ed.). [Online]. New York: New York University Press. Available from: https://dtl.idm.oclc.org/login?url=https://search.credoreference.com/content/entry/nyupencyjud/prophets_and_prophecy/0?institutionId=8909 [Accessed 15 February 2021].

look into the future and to give a direction to the people of God.

Ayto draws from Word origins from Word Origins: 'A prophet is etymologically someone who 'speaks for' another. The word comes via Old French prophete and Latin pmphēta from Greek prophētēs, a compound noun formed from the prefix pro- 'for' and -phētēs 'speaker' (a derivative of phánai 'speak', which goes back to the same Indo-European base, *bha- 'speak', as produced English fable, fate, etc). It meant literally 'spokesman', and was frequently used specifically for 'one who interprets the will of the gods to humans'. The Greek translators of the Bible adopted it into Christian usage. Prophecy [13] comes ultimately from the Greek derivative prophētíā.'[135] This indicates that prophets spoke on behalf of God. They actually acted as transmitters of God's messages. This calls for accuracy in communicating God's messages. It is a shame that many people call themselves prophets when they don't communicate the message from God instead they use prophesy as a way manipulating their audience. I wonder if God would charge a prize to those that receive His message as many that claim to be operating in this office do today. Many use the office of a prophet to communicate their own agendas. It was the purpose of Jesus Christ to keep in touch with those that would build up his church even after his ascension, so he chose to use prophets in this office.

Eph 4:13-16 (NKJV)

---

[135] Prophet. (2006). In J. Ayto, Word origins. (2nd ed.). [Online]. London: A&C Black. Available from: https://dtl.idm.oclc.org/login?url=https://search.credoreference.com/content/entry/acbwordorig/prophet/0?institutionId=8909 [Accessed 17 February 2021].

'And this until we all come into the unity of the faith and of the knowledge of the Son of God, to a full-grown man, to the measure of the stature of the fullness of Christ so that we no longer may be infants, tossed to and fro and carried about by every wind of doctrine, in the dishonesty of men, in cunning craftiness, to the wiles of deceit. But that you, speaking the truth in love, may in all things grow up to Him who is the Head, even Christ.'[136] Coming to the unity of faith may denote, 'until all believers in Christ become united' of which the fact that we haven't come to that point yet means that these five-fold ministry gifts are still in operation.

Bruce affirms: 'This "unity of the faith" is not so much the fact that there is "one faith" (emphasized in verse 5) as the unity among believers which is produced by their common sharing of "the knowledge of the Son of God." Each individual Christian ought to grow up into spiritual maturity, but spiritual maturity in the individual Christian is not enough: there must be spiritual maturity in the corporate personality of the church. And one indispensable prerequisite for such corporate maturity is spiritual unity. Paul has already spoken of "the unity of the Spirit" in verse 3, and it is no different unity that he has in mind here, although he describes it in terms which draw attention to some of its outstanding features. The "unity of the faith" to which he desires his readers to attain, along with himself, depends not simply on the initial act of faith by which one enters into the family of God, but on that ever-increasing appreciation of all that is involved in Christian faith for living and thinking. And this appreciation is best reached in fellowship with one another.'[137] This emphasizes the need for unity as the boy

---

[136] Eph 4:13-16(NKJV)
[137] Chapter 4. (2012). In F. Bruce, *The epistle to the ephesians*.

of Christ in order to achieve full maturity in Christianity. This is a challenge to the church in the post-modernism era where each denomination seems to be seeking and building their own glory competitively to other denominations.

Bruce further proclaims: 'Each part of the body will function as it ought while it is under the control of the head; if it escapes from this control and tries to act independently, the result is very distressing. So it is under the control of Christ that the members of his Church function harmoniously together, sharing his life and attaining maturity under his fostering care, supplied with nourishment and fitted together by means of the "joints and ligaments" (cf. Colossians 2:19). The phrase "fitly framed" is a rendering of the Greek verb *synarmologeo*,which we have already noted in Ephesians 2:21 (its only other New Testament occurrence), where it is used of the harmonious construction of the Church as "a holy temple in the Lord."[138] This means that when we work together as the church of God, we actually we make ourselves more effective in our own callings. We cannot attain excellence in our own individual calling when we work selfishly independently from other Christians.

[Online]. Nashville: Kingsley Books, Inc. Available from: https://dtl.idm.oclc.org/login?url=https://search.credoreference.com/content/entry/ccltdepistle/chapter_4/0?institutionId=8909 [Accessed 19 February 2021].
[138]Chapter 4. (2012). In F. Bruce, *The epistle to the ephesians*. [Online]. Nashville: Kingsley Books, Inc. Available from: https://dtl.idm.oclc.org/login?url=https://search.credoreference.com/content/entry/ccltdepistle/chapter_4/0?institutionId=8909 [Accessed 19 February 2021].

Verse 15: but speaking truth in love, may grow up in all things into him, which is the head, even Christ;

Drawing from RV Margin, Bruce asserts: 'The verb *aletheuo* in this context probably means not only speaking truth but living and acting it as well - "dealing truly," as RV margin puts it.'[139] This means that it is not useless to know or speak of the Christian walk when we don't practice it ourselves.

"**grow up into the head**," Again Bruce asserts: 'Knox Mgr. R.A. Knox pointed out that a baby's head is very large in relation to his body, and that his body, as it develops, is really growing up more and more into a due proportion with the head. Whether this sort of analogy was in Paul's mind or not, it serves as a pleasing illustration of his teaching here. It is by growing up to match the head that the body of Christ - the believing community - attains "the measure of the stature of the fulness of Christ."'[140] This motivates believers to strive for the transformation of our lives to be like Christ and to have the passion he had to please God.

---

[139] Chapter 4. (2012). In F. Bruce, *The epistle to the ephesians*. [Online]. Nashville: Kingsley Books, Inc. Available from: https://dtl.idm.oclc.org/login?url=https://search.credoreference.com/content/entry/ccltdepistle/chapter_4/0?institutionId=8909 [Accessed 19 February 2021].

[140] Chapter 4. (2012). In F. Bruce, *The epistle to the ephesians*. [Online]. Nashville: Kingsley Books, Inc. Available from: https://dtl.idm.oclc.org/login?url=https://search.credoreference.com/content/entry/ccltdepistle/chapter_4/0?institutionId=8909 [Accessed 19 February 2021].

Again Paul uses the illustration of a fully grown up man as an example of spiritual maturity. This does not mean that woman are not included in Paul's illustration as both man and women can be referred to as mankind. Kids are immature in their actions as they can be easily trust which makes them vulnerable so are the Christians who are not mature in the things of God as they can easily be misled. Paul is encouraging the believers not to be afraid to correct each other in love. It is easy to accept a correction from someone whom one who corrects out of love. Correction from a person known of hatred faces a great resistance even if it may be genuine. The five -fold ministry was given by Jesus at his ascension not for individual benefit but for the benefit of the entire body of Christ. It takes maturity and understanding for the body of Christ to start combining their resources together for the building of the kingdom of God as no one should be take pride in building their own kingdom. We cannot all be evangelists but we can help each other and use the gift of evangelism from anyone for the building of God's kingdom.

Guzik draws from the works of Clarke: 'When the gifted offices work right and the saints are properly equipped, Christian maturity increases and there is greater intimacy in the experience of God. c. To a perfect man, to the measure of the stature of the fullness of Christ: The gifted offices and equipped saints bring the saints to maturity, according to the measure of Jesus Himself. As years pass by, we should not only grow old in Jesus, but more mature in Him as well, as both individuals and as a corporate body. d. We should no longer be children, tossed to and fro and carried about with every wind of doctrine: The gifted offices and equipped saints result in stability, being firmly planted on the foundation of the apostles and prophets (Ephesians 2:20). i. Those who do not mature in this way are targets of deceivers, who are effective precisely because they operate with trickery and cunning craftiness – and they lie in wait to deceive. They are out there like land minds that the mature can avoid. ii. The ancient Greek word for tossed to and fro is from the same words used to describe the stormy Sea of Galilee in Luke 8:24 (raging of the water). We can wrongly value movement over growth; mere movement is being tossed to and fro, but God wants us to grow up in all things. iii. By the trickery of men: "The words… refer to the arts used by gamesters, who employ false dice that will always throw up one kind of number, which is that by which those who play with them cannot win." (Clarke) Running after spiritual fads always leaves one a loser.'[141] This indicates the purpose of God for the church that it may grow in unity and in sound doctrine. It is when all gifts function co-operatively that the church can be fully equipped in all areas. It is because of spiritual immaturity that people pursue every doctrine that is not rooted in the word of God. There is a danger of some trying to modernize the ways of God and this resulting to era and compromise of the standards of Christianity. When God's standards are compromised the Church loses spiritual power.

Bray draws from Ridley: 'The church is edified when it is instructed in true faith and good works approved by God, all erroneous opinions, superstitions, errors and heresies put away and is destroyed by false opinions, superstitiousness, evil judgments, errors and heresies of ministers in the church that serve not for the edification of the body of Christ.'[142] This illustrates the need to build up

---

[141] David Guzik(2021),(enduring Word Bible Commentary Ephesians)(OnlineBible Commentary) Available: https://enduringword.com/bible-commentary/Ephesians-4/ Accessed 17/02/2021

[142] Bray, Gerald L., ed. *Galatians, Ephesians*. (Downers Grove:

the church and to safeguard it from false opinions that leads to its destruction.

Eph 4:17-23 (NKJV)

'This I say therefore, and testify in the Lord, that you should not walk from now on as other nations walk, in the vanity of their mind, having the understanding darkened, being alienated from the life of God through the ignorance that is in them, because of the blindness of their heart. For they, being past feeling, have given themselves up to lust, to work all uncleanness with greediness. But you have not so learned Christ, if indeed you have heard Him and were taught by Him, as the truth is in Jesus. For you ought to put off the old man (according to your way of living before) who is corrupt according to the deceitful lusts, and be renewed in the spirit of your mind.'[143]

Elaborating further, Bruce asserts: *'in the vanity of their mind,* So in Romans 1:21, in his grim portrayal of the pagan world, Paul says that in consequence of their failure to acknowledge God, men "became vain in their reasonings." Vanity in the New Testament is sometimes closely associated with idolatry, eg in Acts 14:15, where the men of Lystra, on the point of offering idolatrous sacrifices, are urged to "turn from these vain things unto the living God."'[144] This means that when we are puffed up in our own psychological or philosophical ideological ways that are against the ways of God , we are actually

---

InterVarsity Press.2011)343
[143] Eph 4:17-19(NKJV)
[144] Chapter 4. (2012). In F. Bruce, *The epistle to the ephesians.* [Online]. Nashville: Kingsley Books, Inc. Available from: https://dtl.idm.oclc.org/login?url=https://search.credoreference.com/content/entry/ccltdepistle/chapter_4/0?institutionId=8909 [Accessed 19 February 2021].

practicing idolatry. We cannot grasp the things of God through human reasoning but this can only be attained by the revelation of the Holy Spirit.

Bruce affirms: '*Verse 20: But ye did not so learn Christ;*

Christ himself is the embodiment of his teaching, so much so that his teaching cannot be learned adequately without our coming to know him. The apostolic preaching, by which converts were made, was the good news of what Jesus did; the apostolic teaching, by which converts were instructed in the Christian life, was based on the teaching and example of Christ. Basic to the apostolic teaching was a plain statement regarding the old vices which were to be abandoned and the new graces which were to be cultivated; this statement was frequently couched in terms of "putting off" the old and "putting on" the new.'[145] This means that Christ embodied the scriptures of which Christian should also embody the word of God by becoming the word of God to those that see us. People should be able to learn what Christianity is all about by looking at the lives of the followers of Christ. It is not about studying theology and acquiring theological knowledge about scriptures but it is about having an experience with Christ. It is a shame that in this post-modern world some study theology only to qualify for a job instead of having an experience of the life of Christ.

Osborne declares: 'There is absolutely no place for worldliness in the Christian life. The saints should "no

---

[145] Chapter 4. (2012). In F. Bruce, *The epistle to the ephesians*. [Online]. Nashville: Kingsley Books, Inc. Available from: https://dtl.idm.oclc.org/login?url=https://search.credoreference.com/content/entry/ccltdepistle/chapter_4/0?institutionId=8909 [Accessed 19 February 2021].

longer live as the Gentiles do." If they are indeed saints, they have been set apart (the meaning of hoi hagioi , "holy [or set apart] people") from the world around them and for God. They in essence no longer belong to that world, and they should quit acting as though they do. In the past the Ephesian Christians had been Gentiles living pagan lives— but that was no longer the case and needed to remain in the past. People who have grown up in adverse circumstances never want to return to the old, sad life they have left behind, and that should be even more true of Christians who have left behind darkness for light. When one is seated with God in the heavenly realms in Christ (2:6), why go back to skulk around the old haunts?[146] This means that as followers of Christ we need to live a live worthy of our calling just as the followers of Christ in Antioch were the first to be called Christians because their lives reflected the life of Christ. I wonder if some of us are worth of the name of title of Christians because of the way we conduct ourselves. It has become common to be politically correct in our day to day lives rather than representing the true holiness. We seem to be very much concerned about what people will say or think about us rather than what God would say. Paul critiques the ungodly way of life among Christians. Paul gives the example worldliness which is lust, greediness and all uncleanness. It is a shame that some people live in sin from Monday through Saturday and yet stand to proclaim holiness.

Osborne further elaborates: 'This is even more true in light of the "futility" of the world's thinking. The term mataiotēs means "meaningless" or "empty," devoid of anything worthwhile and entirely the product of a vain

---

[146] Osborne, Grant R. *Ephesians Verse by Verse*. (Oak Harbor: Lexham Press.2017)93

mind. If we apply this to our own situation, we can see that the American way of narcissistic hedonism has no redeeming value whatsoever and is a complete waste. The end product is vacuity, a complete absence of any true satisfaction, and a lifestyle that can never produce anything of benefit. The only viable Christian reaction is a refusal to participate in such errant thinking and actions. Our mindset determines our actions, so if our thinking is empty our lives will be as well.'[147] This explains new ways of thinking in this post- modernism, a generation that believes in experiencing situations before believing. This is a generation that does not believe in the truthfulness of the scriptures instead they rely more on facts rather than the scriptures as the true word of God. In fact this is a more philosophical minded generation that is based in logical ideological principles. Faith in the truthfulness of scripture considered as fanatic and insanity.

Bray further affirms : 'Human beings are born in sin, and therefore by nature they are unable to do anything that is truly good. The world around us is thoroughly corrupt, and to think the way it does is to share in that corruption. Before we were converted that was inevitable, but Christians have had their eyes opened to the truth and must now change their behavior accordingly. This means leaving aside everything that belonged to the old life and putting on an entirely new one. It is not just a question of outward acts but of those inward thoughts and convictions on which those outward acts are based. We were created in the image of God, but that image was ruined by the fall of Adam and now has to be painstakingly restored in Christ.'[148] This is a call to a complete change of mind and

---

[147] Osborne, Grant R. *Ephesians Verse by Verse*. (Oak Harbor: Lexham Press.2017)94
[148] Bray, Gerald L., ed. *Galatians, Ephesians*. (Downers Grove:

a change of behaviour. (Metanoea in Greek) which is a change of mind, a change of attitude, change of behaviour and a change of direction. We cannot claim that we repented and are saved when we still walk the same way in an ungodly manner. Otherwise it this born again experience that qualifies us for eternal life as Children of God as Luke proclaims: 'I tell you, no; but unless you repent [change your old way of thinking, turn from your sinful ways and live changed lives], you will all likewise perish. I tell you, no; but unless you repent [change your old way of thinking, turn from your sinful ways and live changed lives], you will all likewise perish.'[149] This emphasizes a need to repent rather than just joining the fellowship of Christians.

Mounce define true repentance Verb : (metanoe), GK 3566 (S 3340), 34x. Both noun and verb denote a radical, moral turn of the whole person from sin and to God. The words themselves are derived from meta ("after") plus nous ("mind, understanding") for the noun or noeo ("to perceive, understand") for the verb.'[150] This means that when we decide to follow Christ we should make a complete turn -around of life.

'Verse 22: that you put off, concerning your former conduct, the old man which grows corrupt according to the deceitful lusts,

Bruce further affirms: 'The old man is what they were before they became Christians, the old Adam which is our natural heritage. In Romans 6:6 Paul enlarges on the

---

InterVarsity Press.2011) 351
[149] Luke 13:3 (AMP)
[150] Mounce, William D., and Zondervan Staff. *Mounce's Complete Expository Dictionary of Old and New Testament Words.* (Grand Rapids: HarperCollins Christian Publishing 2006)800

meaning of baptism, in which Christians are "buried" with Christ and thus "united with him by the likeness of his death," by affirming that "our old man was crucified with him." In Colossians 3:9 he reminds his readers that they "have put off the old man with his doings." But in the present passage Christians, who (in the sense of these quotations from other epistles) have already had their "old man" crucified with Christ and so have already "put him off," are exhorted to put him off. The Christian ethic in the New Testament presents a remarkable blend of the indicative and the imperative moods; it might be summed up in the words: "Be what you are" - "Be in practice what you are by divine calling!" God had called these people out of the old life into the new, and this transition had been symbolized in their baptism, at the very threshold of their Christian career; but the significance of their baptism must be spelt out in daily living. Let that daily living proclaim as eloquently in one way what their baptism had proclaimed in another way: their decisive farewell to all that they had formerly been. This tension between the indicative and the imperative arises from the fact that while the believer is spiritually united to Christ at God's right hand and belongs to the age to come, yet temporally, so long as he remains in mortal body, he lives on earth and is involved in this present age.'[151] Just as water baptism acts as a public declaration of death to the sinful way of life and the resurrection in the newness of life. So Christians should display their new way of life by living in holiness rather than progressing with their old ways of living.

---

[151] Chapter 4. (2012). In F. Bruce, *The epistle to the ephesians*. [Online]. Nashville: Kingsley Books, Inc. Available from: https://dtl.idm.oclc.org/login?url=https://search.credoreference.com/content/entry/ccltdepistle/chapter_4/0?institutionId=8909 [Accessed 19 February 2021].

Eph 4:24-32 (NKJV)

'And you should put on the new man, who according to God was created in righteousness and true holiness. Therefore putting away lying, let each man speak truth with his neighbour, for we are members of one another. Be angry, and do not sin. Do not let the sun go down upon your wrath, neither give place to the Devil. Let him who stole steal no more, but rather let him labour, working with his hands the thing which is good, so that he may have something to give to him who needs. Let not any filthy word go out of your mouth, but if any is good to building up in respect of need, that it may give grace to the ones hearing. And do not grieve the Holy Spirit of God, by whom you are sealed until the day of redemption. Let all bitterness and wrath and anger and tumult and evil speaking be put away from you, with all malice. And be kind to one another, tender-hearted, forgiving one another, even as God for Christ's sake has forgiven you.'[152] I wonder if Paul considered that a person is not defined by what they may be wearing but by their personality. May be Paul could have emphasized repentance and becoming a new man rather than putting on as it may be misinterpreted for the outward performance or pretending rather than living a true life of holiness.

Paul advices the Christians not let the sun go down in their anger probably because demons are associated with night and darkness. When one is asleep they do not have control of their mind which may be the battleground of demons. When one goes to bed angry, they are likely to

---

[152] Eph 4:24-32 (NKJV)

have nightmares in their sleep which is a sign of the attack of the devil.

'*Verse 26:: Be angry, and do not sin"*

Bruce goes on proclaiming: 'This is a verbal reproduction of the opening words of Psalm 4:4 in the Septuagint version; AV and RV render the Massoretic (Hebrew) text by "Stand in awe, and sin not." The Hebrew verb *ragaz* may denote a variety of emotional disturbances, including trembling with fear or anger. In RSV the opening words of Psalm 4:4 are rendered "Be angry, but sin not." What Paul means by this admonition is made plain by his following words. It is not sinful to be angry, but it is all too easy to let anger run to excess through lack of control, and righteous indignation may degenerate into sinful resentment, and can even become the first step on the road that leads to murder. Hence our Lord's solemn words about being angry with one's brother in Matthew 5:22. "Be angry without sinning," says Paul. But how? By exercising a firm control over one's anger, and limiting its duration.'[153] This does not justify be temperamental as the scriptures compare a person who have no self-control to a city without walls. As Christians filled by the Holy Spirit, we should be able to birth self control with us. But we remain human even when we become Christians of which we can be angry at times and still remain with the ability to control our temper rather than being controlled by our temper. Uncontrolled anger births sin in our lives and we even become insensitive to

---

[153]Chapter 4. (2012). In F. Bruce, *The epistle to the ephesians*. [Online]. Nashville: Kingsley Books, Inc. Available from: https://dtl.idm.oclc.org/login?url=https://search.credoreference.com/content/entry/ccltdepistle/chapter_4/0?institutionId=8909 [Accessed 19 February 2021].

the voice of God who usually communed with Adam in the quiet times of the early morning.

Verse 27: (YLT) 'neither give place to the devil.'

Bruce goes on asserting: 'Those who nurse their wrath to keep it warm may not realize that they are giving the devil a golden opportunity to exploit their cherished indignation to gain his own ends. But he must be allowed no room, not the slightest foothold, within the Christian's life. The term *diabolos* ("slanderer"), the Greek equivalent of the Hebrew *satan* ("adversary"), is found in the Pauline writings only in Ephesians and in the Pastoral Epistles (cf. Ephesians 6:11); Paul normally prefers to use *satanas*, the Hebrew word supplied with a Greek termination.'[154] This indicates that the devil is a chancier and that he gains a grip on us when we nurse anger within us and he uses that opportunity to falsely accuse us. The devil speaks to a person's conscience as that individual keep their thoughts in the wrong.

Wolfgang affirms: 'Paul makes good use of the words "put on." He compares the external appearance of our life with a garment that, for better or worse, covers our body and in which we live and move in the eyes of other people. The condition of our life and behaviour is just like that. We wear it like a garment and so move in society either decently or shamefully. In German we say, "You must put another dress on," by which we mean that you must change the way you live. Changing clothes is easy,

---

[154]Chapter 4. (2012). In F. Bruce, *The epistle to the ephesians*. [Online]. Nashville: Kingsley Books, Inc. Available from: https://dtl.idm.oclc.org/login?url=https://search.credoreference.com/content/entry/ccltdepistle/chapter_4/0?institutionId=8909 [Accessed 19 February 2021].

and we all do it on special occasions, but you will find very few people who think, when they put on different clothes, that they are being reminded by this that they need to change their entire way of life. We are embarrassed if there are blots on our clothes but not if there are blots on our life; we dress well but live shamefully. The smell of our clothes is good, but right next to it is the putrid stench of our life, which is hardly compatible with our claims to be Christian.'[155] This challenges us to constantly check ourselves through the scriptures and to change our ways of life on a daily basis as we do change our clothes daily. At times the clothes may appear clean yet they have a bad smell. Same applies to our lives that may appear good from our own perspective yet others will be seeing all bad things about us. It is also good to learn to listen to advice from others as we might be blind to our own smell or evil manners.

Dickson asserts: 'The doctrine of Christ expressly requires of believers that they perform these three things: (1) That following repentance, they should more and more put off and lay aside the old person, or that corrupt nature that showed itself in their former conversation, which corrupt nature or old person is daily made worse and more corrupt through deceitful lusts, and so it more and more corrupts and destroys people. (2) That they should be more and more renewed in the spirit of their mind, that is, that believers should do their endeavor, through the Word and Spirit of God, to make their understanding more and more spiritual, which of its own nature is repugnant to the wisdom of God and argues against it. (3) That believers should put on the new person or should study to manifest and declare in themselves the actions and qualities of the

---

[155] Bray, Gerald L., ed. *Galatians, Ephesians*. (Downers Grove: InterVarsity Press.2011)356

new creature, renewed after the image of God, and therefore should carefully yield obedience to the divine law in those things that respect God and their neighbor. Hence the argument is thus: the Christian doctrine requires of you that putting off the manners of the old person, your mind being renewed, you should study to approve yourselves new creatures, in the exercise of righteousness and holiness. Therefore you should not walk as other Gentiles.'[156] This affirms the fact that Christians should reflect a changed way of life in terms of speech, fidelity, mentality and their general way of life. This means that their way of life should match Christianity that which they claim to be.

Eph 4:29(NKJV)

' **Let no corrupt word proceed out of your mouth, but what is good for necessary edification, that it may impart grace to the hearers.**'[157] Bruce avows: 'In Colossians 4:6 Paul says that Christian speech should always be "seasoned with salt." Otherwise it may become insipid, or even worse; it may become both corrupt and corrupting. Foul language had no doubt been habitual with many of his readers before they became Christians; but such language is most unbecoming in a Christian. It must, therefore, be renounced. But the absence of such "colorful" embellishments of talk (as they are sometimes accounted) does not mean that one's talk will become colorless. Just as the command to steal no more is followed by the positive injunction to be generous, so here the prohibition of harmful talk is accompanied by the inculcation of helpful talk. It is recorded of R.C.

---

[156]Bray, Gerald L., ed. *Galatians, Ephesians.* (Downers Grove: InterVarsity Press.2011)356
[157] Eph 4:29(NKJV)

Chapman's home in Barnstaple: "There was great cheerfulness at the table - words of wisdom and grace were constantly heard; but no room was given for conversation to degenerate into frivolous talk. It was also a rule of the house that no one should speak ill of an absent person, and any infringement of this rule called forth a firm though gracious reproof." Conversation with a view to timely instruction will help to build up a strong Christian character and stimulate growth in grace.'[158] This means that as Christians we should maintain a certain way of conversation that does not glorify Christ. I personally was surprised by some Christians in a particular culture who had adopted the world ways of making jokes where people no longer have the ability to complete each of their communication without including 'f' words. Swearing has become a normal way of communication. Paul was warning the believers of Ephesus never to get caught up in this kind of life which doesn't portray the life of Christ.

Eph 4: 3-30 (NKJV)

And do not grieve the Holy Spirit of God, by whom you were sealed for the day of redemption.'[159]

Bruce further elaborates: 'The Holy Spirit of God is here spoken of personally, as capable of being grieved. The implication is that unedifying language grieves the Spirit who dwells in the speaker and the hearer alike, for it tends to break down that common life in the body of

---

[158] Chapter 4. (2012). In F. Bruce, *The epistle to the ephesians*. [Online]. Nashville: Kingsley Books, Inc. Available from: https://dtl.idm.oclc.org/login?url=https://search.credoreference.com/content/entry/ccltdepistle/chapter_4/0?institutionId=8909 [Accessed 19 February 2021].

[159] Eph 4:30 (NkJV)

Christ which it is the Spirit's province to maintain. To grieve one's brother or cause him to stumble (Romans 14:15,21) is an offense against the Christian fellowship and therefore against the Spirit himself. Paul has already reminded his readers (Ephesians 1:13 f.) that when they believed they received the seal of the Spirit, as a pledge of the inheritance which would be theirs on the day when God claimed them finally as his own possession, as a universal demonstration of his glory. That is the "day of redemption" referred to here, the day of "the revealing of the sons of God" (Romans 8:19), the day of Christ's coming "to be glorified in his saints, and to be marvelled at in all them that believed" (2 Thessalonians 1:10).'[160] This explains that the Holy Spirit have the attributes of a person as he can be grieved as humans. It grieves the Holy Spirit for the humans to dwell in sin knowing that the our bodies are the temples of the Holy Spirit. It is true that each one of us once had their conscience telling them not to do a certain thing but we often ignore that still voice from within. As we continue violating the will of the Holy Spirit as Human he can get offended and live us and we remain sinning without a conscience speaking from within facilitating our way to condemnation.

Eph 4:31(YLT)

Let all bitterness, and wrath, and anger, and clamour, and evil-speaking, be put away from you, with all malice,'[161]

---

[160]Chapter 4. (2012). In F. Bruce, *The epistle to the ephesians*. [Online]. Nashville: Kingsley Books, Inc. Available from: https://dtl.idm.oclc.org/login?url=https://search.credoreference.com/content/entry/ccltdepistle/chapter_4/0?institutionId=8909 [Accessed 19 February 2021].

All forms of maliciousness and ill-will must be abandoned from our Christian lives. These include: temper, unrestricted quarrelling and malicious whispers and many other.

Eph 4:32(YLT)

'and become one to another kind, tender-hearted, forgiving one another, according as also God in Christ did forgive you.'[162]

Elaborating further Bruce asserts:'Mutual kindness, compassion, and a readiness to forgive are the qualities which should characterize Christians. Most appropriately so; for they were the qualities which characterized Christ. Moreover, he ascribed these same qualities to God, and made that fact the chief reason why the children of God should exhibit them. By the exercise of love and forgiveness, he told his disciples, "ye shall be sons of the Most High: for he is kind toward the unthankful and evil. Be ye merciful, even as your Father is merciful" (Luke 6:35 f.). And it is the forgiving grace of God that Paul invokes here - more especially, his forgiving grace manifested in Christ - as the crowning incentive towards a spirit of forgiveness in his children. Those who have been forgiven so much, and at so great a cost, must be forgiving in their turn. So too our Lord taught his disciples to pray, "Forgive us our trespasses as we forgive them that trespass against us" - not because our forgiving others can be the ground of God's free forgiveness of us, but because we can neither seek nor enjoy his forgiveness so long as we cherish an unforgiving spirit to others (Matthew 6:12,14 f.; 18:21-35).'[163] This explains that as Christian

---

[161] Eph 4:31 (YLT)
[162] Eph 4:32(YLT)

we should demonstrate the life of love, kindness, compassion and forgives.

Eph 5:1 (NKJV)

'Therefore be imitators of God as dear children.

Thielman asserts: 'The notion of imitating God was a major theme in Plato, who uses the verb μιμέομαι to explain how human beings, who exist in the real world, can be assimilated to God, who exists in the world of ideas. This was primarily a mental exercise—"no more than reflection on the image of the god retained in the memory," as Michaelis puts it (TDNT 4:661)—but occasionally Plato developed the idea of assimilation to God in an ethical direction. People should flee from the earthly realm, he says, where evils hover in the air and should "become like God [ὁμοίωσις θεῷ] as far as possible; and to become like God is to become righteous and holy [δίκαιον καὶ ὅσιον] and wise " (Plato, Theaet. 176a– b, trans. Fowler 1921; cf. Eph. 4:24). 19 These ideas reappear in Hellenistic philosophers and moralists in later years (e.g., Epictetus [Arrian, Epict. diss. 2.14.12]), including first-century Hellenistic'[164] This is calling for a life of holiness among Christians. God is a holy God and being the imitators of God is repositioning ourselves to the presence of God where the first men fell from because of

---

[163] Chapter 4. (2012). In F. Bruce, *The epistle to the ephesians*. [Online]. Nashville: Kingsley Books, Inc. Available from: https://dtl.idm.oclc.org/login?url=https://search.credoreference.com/content/entry/ccltdepistle/chapter_4/0?institutionId=8909 [Accessed 19 February 2021].
[164] Thielman, Frank. *Ephesians* (Baker Exegetical Commentary on the New Testament). Grand Rapids: Baker Academic.2010)324.

sin. It is a shame that science and human reasoning can never understand or explain God as Plato, Hellenistic philosophers and moralists tried to do.

Mounce elaborates: 'IMITATE, IMITATOR New Testament Verb : (mimeomai) GK 3628 (S 3401), 4x. mimeomai means "to imitate." Noun : (mim t s) GK 3629 (S 3402), 6x. mim t s means "imitator." In the early church, many new believers needed models to show them how to live a redeemed lifestyle, since up to that time their lives were shaped by a pagan culture. John informs his audience, "Do not imitate what is evil but what is good" (3 Jn. 11). The author of Hebrews suggests that believers use their leaders as "examples" (Heb. 13:7; cf. 6:12). Paul acknowledges that the Thessalonians have used Paul and company as their examples (1 Thess. 1:6; 2 Thess. 3:7, 9. In fact, Paul does not hesitate to instruct his churches to "imitate" him (1 Cor. 4:16; 11:1). But Paul says this only because he feels deeply that he himself is following the example of Christ the Lord (11:1; Eph. 5:1).'[165] This may explain that the believers of Ephesus did not need to struggle what it meant to imitate God as they had Paul as a model of godliness. All they needed to do was to follow the example of Paul in their daily walk with Christ. This is a challenge to all Christian leaders to live a live worthy emulating.

Swindol asserts: 'The Greek word translated "imitators" is mimētēs [3402], from which we derive our English word "mimic." When we mimic somebody, we act out what they're doing; we follow their lead, trying to copy their actions. But how can we possibly mimic God's actions? This would be an incredibly daunting challenge if

---

[165] Mounce, William D., and Zondervan Staff. Mounce's *Complete Expository Dictionary of Old and New Testament Words.* (Grand Rapids: HarperCollins Christian Publishing.2006)498

it were not for Paul's next phrase: "as beloved children." In other words, as members of His spiritual family, we should take after our heavenly Father.'[166] This may be a call for Christian to dwell on the scriptures from which we find the ways of God.

Eph 5:2 (NKJV)

'And walk in love, as Christ also has loved us and given Himself for us, an offering and a sacrifice to God for a sweet-smelling aroma.'[167]

Swindoll proclaims: 'Paul also illustrates the extent of our imitation. We are to walk in "love"—unconditional agapē love. The example? Christ's self- sacrificial love by which He gave Himself up for us, thus pleasing God as "a fragrant aroma" (5:2). Paul presents us with the greatest standard of selfless love, just as Jesus Himself taught: "Greater love has no one than this, that one lay down his life for his friends" (John 15:13). As one commentator notes, "He is telling us to love our neighbors in the sense of being willing to work for their well-being even if it means sacrificing our own well- being to that end." Therefore from Paul's perspectivebeing like God is walking in love. It is in human mechanism to love those that love us and to treat well those that treat us well too but the love of God is the agape love, the unmerited type of love, the love that loves unconditionally. It is the love that gives without expecting anything in return just as God so loved the world that He gave his own son to atone for the sins of the world.

---

[166] Swindoll, Charles R. *Insights on Galatians, Ephesians.* (Carol Stream: Tyndale House Publishers. 2015)265
[167] Eph 5:2(NKJV)

Eph 5:3-5(NKJV)

'But fornication and all uncleanness or covetousness, let it not even be named among you, as is fitting for saints; neither filthiness, nor foolish talking, nor coarse jesting, which are not fitting, but rather giving of thanks.' For this you know, that no fornicator, unclean person, nor covetous man, who is an idolater, has any inheritance in the kingdom of Christ and God.'[168] Paul wanted it to be very clear that sarcastic ridicule, whoredom, and all uncleanness, or covetousness are not acceptable among Christians and that such people will not inherit the Kingdom of God. It is a shame that we now live in a work of deception when people justify sin even through scriptures. I have head of people who refer to the story of David and Bathsheba and that he remained a man after God's heart even after the sin of idolatry.The truth is that God is holy and He does not tolerate sin in his presence from anyone but at the same time God is a gracious God that forgives sin if one repent as David did repent of his sin although God punished him in the death of his son.Heil affirms: 'On "sexual immorality" (pornei&a) O'Brien (Ephesians , 359 n. 2) notes: "The pornei&a word-group was employed in the lxx to denote unchastity, harlotry, prostitution, and fornication. In later rabbinic literature the noun was understood to include not only prostitution and any kind of extramarital sexual intercourse, but also all marriages between relatives forbidden by rabbinic law. Incest and all kinds of unnatural sexual intercourse were regarded as fornication (pornei&a)."'[169]This explains that sexual immorality was a broad phrase that included any form of prostitution, sex

---

[168] Eph 5:3-5(NKJV)
[169] Heil, John Paul. 2007. Ephesians : Empowerment to Walk in Love for the Unity of All in Christ. Atlanta: Society of Biblical Literature.

outside marriage, incest, homosexuality and many other forms of unnatural sex. I wonder if this word still carries the same meaning for our postmodern generation that seem to be compromising the preaching of the gospel to remain within the margins of political correctness. One has to be very careful not to offend the other person because of their comments.

The amplified makes it even clearer: 'But sexual immorality and all [moral] impurity [indecent, offensive behavior] or greed must not even be hinted at among you, as is proper among saints [for as believers our way of life, whether in public or in private, reflects the validity of our faith]. 4 Let there be no filthiness and silly talk, or coarse [obscene or vulgar] joking, *because* such things are not appropriate [for believers]; but instead speak of your thankfulness [to God]. 5 For be sure of this: no immoral, impure, or greedy person—for that one is [in effect] an idolater—has any inheritance in the kingdom of Christ and God [for such a person places a higher value on something other than God].'[170]

Swindoll further declares: 'Paul begins with two deeds that relate to sexual sin. The first, "immorality," translates the Greek word porneia [4202], which shares a common root with our word "pornography." It includes all kinds of sexual sin outside of marriage, including fornication, adultery, homosexuality, and prostitution. While these outward actions should all be avoided, in the Sermon on the Mount Christ focused attention even more pointedly at their inward source—the lust that He said was tantamount to committing adultery in the heart (Matt. 5:28). Paul also refers to "impurity," using the Greek word akatharsia [167], which is related to our English word "catharsis" but

---

[170] Eph 5:3-5(AMP)

formed as a negative. Just as something cathartic cleanses us, something "akathartic" pollutes us. Thus, akatharsia refers to the effects of immorality on our hearts, minds, and bodies— moral uncleanness that leads to guilt, shame, habitual sin, obsessions, addictions, and a life that spirals out of control.[171] This means that God demands total or complete purity even from our way of thinking as well as in our daily physical conduct. It is a great tragedy that our present world actually defends impurity and wickedness

Eph 5:6-7 (AMP)

' Let no one deceive you with empty arguments [that encourage you to sin], for because of these things the wrath of God comes upon the sons of disobedience [those who habitually sin So do not participate *or* even associate with them [in the rebelliousness of sin]'[172] This is an elaboration of the fact that there are preachers who justify and defend sexual immoral life using some theological or philosophical arguments to convince people. Some believe in what they call free expression of which they teach that sex talk is harmless or even healthy as they assume that nobody gets offended but Paul warns us not to be deceived by these that rationalise sin. Paul makes it clear that such people and those that take hid of their deceitful teachings cause the wrath of God. I wonder what God does in his wrath but in the wilderness when the children of Israel caused the anger of God through idolatry and murmuring and their disobedience to Moses, the bible reminds us how serpents came in to bite people and how the earth was open and some were swallowed up. I wonder if the

---

[171]Swindoll, Charles R.. *Insights on Galatians, Ephesians*. Carol Stream: Tyndale House Publishers. 2015)266
[172] Eph 5:6-7(AMP)

pandemic, and many more natural disasters can be God's way of communicating with this present generation.

Swindoll further affirms: 'The phrase "silly talk" is one compound word in Greek: mōrologia [3473] . From its root we derive the English word "moron," which means "fool." It's not a stretch to translate this colloquially as "talking like a moron." In Scripture, fool doesn't primarily refer to a person lacking intellectual ability but to somebody who denies the reality of God. David wrote, "The fool has said in his heart, 'There is no God'" (Ps. 14:1). Historically, mōros [3474] pointed to "a practical denial of God as the Judge of good and evil." 7 Mōrologia refers to pointless, empty, and foolish talk— unnecessary verbiage that's neither profitable nor edifying.'[173] This means that as Christians we should not worst time participating in the ungodly conversations. In actual fact such ungodly conversations actually sucks out godliness from Christians. This does not mean that Christians should not have humour but we should not cross our boundaries as Christians.

Eph 5:8-13 (YLT)

' for ye were once darkness, and now light in the Lord; as children of light walk ye, for the fruit of the Spirit is in all goodness, and righteousness, and truth, proving what is well-pleasing to the Lord, and have no fellowship with the unfruitful works of the darkness and rather even convict, for the things in secret done by them it is a shame even to speak of, and all the things reproved by the light are manifested, for everything that is manifested is light;'[174]

---

[173] Swindoll, Charles R. *Insights on Galatians, Ephesians*.2015)267
[174] Eph 5:8-13(YLT)

Swindoll further asserts: 'Formerly darkness, now light— that's the new identity for all believers in Christ from the moment they place their faith in Him. As light-bearers who reflect God's perfect light of holiness, truth, love, and hope, we are urged to point the way for others to escape the darkness. To do this, we need to "walk as children of Light" (5:8). What does this look like? Paul describes it as producing goodness, righteousness, and truth (5:9). We depart from the former ways described in 5:3-5. Instead, pleasing the Lord becomes our life ambition (5:10). Paul describes here a complete reorienting of our lives, a turning away from the path of darkness and advancing on the path of life— all set in motion and empowered by the grace of God through the power of the Holy Spirit.'[175]. This means that as Christians we should be the problem solvers rather than being the problem ourselves to our communities as Matthew asserted in Matthew 5:14-16 (RSV) 'You are the light of the world. A city set on a hill cannot be hid. Nor do men light a lamp and put it under a bushel, but on a stand, and it gives light to all in the house. Let your light so shine before men, that they may see your good works and give glory to your Father who is in heaven.'[176] This is a challenge to Christians to live a life that is exemplary to the world. It is being a problem when Christians break the laws of the government. Paul seems to be highlighting the fact that before salvation the Ephesians believers were themselves the problem of which it has to change as they now had a new identity in Christ which is light. Paul is highlighting the fact that most Christians do very disgraceful things behind their closed doors. I am reminded of one Christian in South Africa who was found

---

[175]Swindoll, Charles R. *Insights on Galatians, Ephesians.*2015)271
[176]Matt 5:14-16(RSV)

dead after she was electrocuted by a faulty electric vibrator.

Eph 5:14-17(RSV)

'Therefore it is said, "Awake, O sleeper, and arise from the dead, and Christ shall give you light."Look carefully then how you walk, not as unwise men but as wise, making the most of the time, because the days are evil. Therefore do not be foolish, but understand what the will of the Lord is.'[177] Paul advices us to redeem the time which is to seize the moment for the glory of Jesus. It is to make the most of our time. Again Swindoll declares : 'With this brief snippet of a chorus, Paul reminds his readers that the dawn of redemption has pushed back the thick cloak of night. A glorious morning has risen in which believers now bask in the brilliant rays of Christ's glory'[178] This is a challenge to start living a life that glorifies Christ. This does not happen on its own as Christians have to pick themselves up and strive for excellence as Solomon proclaims: Proverbs 24:16 (AMP) 'For a righteous man falls seven times, and rises again, But the wicked stumble in *time of* disaster *and* collapse.'[179] This means that it is pointless to complain about your failures and still do nothing to get yourself better.

Eph 5:18-21 (YLT)

'and be not drunk with wine, in which is dissoluteness, but be filled in the Spirit, speaking to yourselves in psalms and hymns and spiritual songs, singing and making melody in your heart to the Lord, giving thanks always for

---

[177] Eph 5:14-17(RSV)
[178] Swindoll, Charles R. *Insights on Galatians, Ephesians*.2015)272
[179] Proverbs 24:16(AMP)

all things, in the name of our Lord Jesus Christ, to the God and Father; subjecting yourselves to one another in the fear of God.'[180]

Swindoll elaborates: 'Paul begins this exhortation with a contrast— being drunk and out of control versus being under the Spirit's control. This is the difference between having our minds depressed and our senses numbed versus having them invigorated and stimulated. People who are controlled by too much alcohol waste their time, squander their resources, and make fools of themselves. When people are drunk, the things they say usually profit no one. Their words are either garbled and slurred nonsense or full of coarse vulgarities. Contrast that with people who are controlled by the Spirit. Their minds are clear to see all that Christ has done and is doing. Their hearts are filled with joy as their lips overflow with praise. The Spirit of God fills their hearts with gratitude as their mouths speak in "psalms and hymns and spiritual songs" (5:19). In fact, their entire lives are directed to God the Father through the Lord Jesus Christ (5:20) and by the power of the Holy Spirit.'[181] This highlights the fact that as Christians we should not be under the influence of alcohol instead we should be filled by the Holy Spirit. Both Holy Spirit make one high but unlike alcohol or drugs the Holy Spirit gives joy and does not lead to crime or violence, physical and mental illness and many more as does alcohol and drugs. Today many people end up with severe mental health problems because of drugs and alcohol. Many people try to escape from the life problems by getting themselves intoxicated without evaluating the after effects .Having known that challenges that the Ephesians believers may be encountering because of their Christianity, Paul

---
[180] Eph 5:10-21(YLT)
[181] Swindoll, Charles R. *Insights on Galatians, Ephesians*.2015)278

discourages them from getting themselves intoxicated but rather to be filled by the Holy Spirit. There are many benefits of being filled by the Holy Spirit that includes: Deepening your relationship with God, Creating a hunger for the things of God, Understanding the word of God, Improved prayer life, Renewal of the mind, Sanctification, Seeing things clearer and many more.

Eph 5:22-33 (KJV)

'Wives, submit to your own husbands, as to the Lord. For the husband is head of the wife, as also Christ is head of the church; and He is the Savior of the body. Therefore, just as the church is subject to Christ, so let the wives be to their own husbands in everything. Husbands, love your wives, just as Christ also loved the church and gave Himself for her, that He might sanctify and cleanse her with the washing of water by the word, that He might present her to Himself a glorious church, not having spot or wrinkle or any such thing, but that she should be holy and without blemish. So husbands ought to love their own wives as their own bodies; he who loves his wife loves himself. For no one ever hated his own flesh, but nourishes and cherishes it, just as the Lord does the church. For we are members of His body, of His flesh and of His bones."For this reason a man shall leave his father and mother and be joined to his wife, and the two shall become one flesh." This is a great mystery, but I speak concerning Christ and the church. Nevertheless let each one of you in particular so love his own wife as himself, and let the wife see that she respects her husband.'[182] Paul

---

[182] Eph 5:22-33(NKJV)

uses a metaphor of the husband and wife to explain the required relationship between Christ and the Church.

Heil proclaims : 'Some (e.g., Lincoln, Ephesians , 366; O'Brien, Ephesians , 404) insist that fo&boj in Eph 5:21 should be translated more strongly as "fear" rather than "respect" or "reverence." But Hoehner (Ephesians , 719) comments that "since the word is used in the context of Christ's love that is so amply demonstrated in this letter, it is best to view it as a reverential fear or reverential respect. This quality of 'fear' motivates believers to submit to others within the body.'"[183]

This means that Paul is not referring to trembling because of the other rather he refers to a reverential fear in honour of Christ. This doesn't give any room to manipulation and abuse of women by man in their relationship but to work together as equal partners recognising that someone has that legitimate authority over you in the building of the family. This does not mean that the wife become inferior to the husband but understanding what Sub- Mission means. A football a sub carries the same value as all other players in the field only that he waits for his time to shine. So it is in marriage. Marriage is a mission of God preaching the love of Christ and the Church. The wife willingly put herself under the mission allowing one to take the lead as they work together.

Swindoll further proclaims: 'Paul says wives are to "be subject to [their] own husbands, as to the Lord" (5:22). In the New American Standard translation, the words "be subject" are in italics. This indicates that the original Greek text does not include these words. But the Greek

---

[183] Heil, John Paul. Ephesians : *Empowerment to Walk in Love for the Unity of All in Christ.* Atlanta: Society of Biblical Literature.2007)241

grammar makes it clear that Paul is simply continuing the thought introduced in 5:21—"be subject to one another in the fear of Christ." The Greek text then says, literally, "The wives to their own husbands" (5:22). Note that Paul is speaking here only about the marriage relationship (wives and husbands), not about the general relationship between men and women. He makes this clear with the Greek word idios [2398] — "your own." Wives are not told to be in submission to every man but to their own husbands.'[184]

This indicates that some women may find it easy to show submission to other man rather than to their own husbands. I have found it common in the African culture that woman would bow before the pastor or any other dignitary as a sign of respect yet they find it very difficult to show such respect to their own husbands. It is also common to bow before the lord which is a good thing to do but Christ in this case is the husband of the Church which is his bride. It is a sign of respect when the Church bows down in worship of the lord but Paul want it to be clear that such respect should also be practiced in our families although this does not make woman less important than man. Paul encourages husbands to respect their wives, recognizing them as valuable gifts from God as Christ seeks to demonstrate his love to the church in the same way the husband have to seek to respect his wife in a way that show his love for her even as Peter stresses in (1 Pet. 3:7).

Guzik draws from Jones: "'Notice that the Apostles lay great stress upon it. Man was created first. But not only that; man was also made the lord of creation. It was to man that this authority was given over the brute animal

---

[184] Charles R. *Insights on Galatians, Ephesians*.2015)283

creation; it was man who was called upon to give them names. Here are indications that man was put into a position of leadership, lordship, and authority and power. He takes the decisions, he gives the rulings. That is the fundamental teaching with regard to this whole matter." (Lloyd-Jones)'[185] This means that the reason for woman submitting to their husband is to honour God's order of things for a woman to be the complement and help for her husband.

According to Guzik the order of things is that : Jesus submitted to His parents (Luke 2:51).

Spiritual forces submitted to the disciples (Luke 10:17).

Citizens should submit to government authority (Romans 13:1 and 5, Titus 3:1, 1 Peter 2:13).

The universe will submit to Jesus (1 Corinthians 15:27 and Ephesians 1:22).

Unseen spiritual beings submit to Jesus (1 Peter 3:22).

Christians should submit to church leaders (1 Corinthians 16:15-16 and Hebrews 13:17).

The church should submit to Jesus (Ephesians 5:24).

Servants should submit to masters (Titus 2:9 and 1 Peter 2:18).

Christians should submit to God (Hebrews 12:9 and James 4:7). And Wives should submit to husbands (Colossians 3:18, Titus 2:5, 1 Peter 3:5, Ephesians 5:22-24

Heil draws from Lincoln: "'The definite article (lit. 'the washing in [the] water') may well indicate a specific event, and the readers are scarcely likely to have taken this as anything other than a reference to their experience of

---

[185]David Guzik(2021),(enduring Word Bible Commentary Ephesians)(OnlineBible Commentary) Available: https://enduringword.com/bible-commentary/Ephesians-5/ Accessed 22/02/2021

baptism. In 1 Cor 6:11 washing and sanctifying occur together as metaphors of salvation, with an allusion to baptism highly probable. But here, the explicit mention of water suggests not simply an extended metaphor for salvation but a direct reference to water baptism, not to baptism by the Spirit. . . . the language of 'the washing with water' is likely to have as a secondary connotation the notion of the bridal bath. This would reflect both Jewish marital customs with their prenuptial bath and the marital imagery of Ezek 16:8– 14 which stands behind this passage. In Ezek 16:9 Yahweh, in entering his marriage covenant with Jerusalem, is said to have bathed her with water and washed off the blood from her.'"[186] This is an elaboration of the atonement sacrifice by Christ to the Church of which man should also demonstrate a sacrificial love for the perfection of his own wife. It is the duty of the husband to buy beautiful clothes and perfumes for their wife although woman can do these things for themselves.

Swindoll goes on elaborating: 'At this point we need to emphasize that in Christ we all have equal dignity, so Paul's statement has nothing to do with inferiority. In Galatians 3:28, Paul says, "There is neither Jew nor Greek, there is neither slave nor free man, there is neither male nor female; for you are all one in Christ Jesus." Such a statement was a profoundly countercultural claim in Paul's day. It was a time when many Jews felt superior to Gentiles, while Gentiles frequently disrespected Jews. Sometimes slave traders considered their wares to be pieces of property, like cattle, whose value was directly linked to their strengths, skills, or abilities. And men often believed that women, who were typically less physically

---

[186]Heil, John Paul. Ephesians *: Empowerment to Walk in Love for the Unity of All in Christ*. Atlanta: Society of Biblical Literature 2007)246

strong than them, were therefore essentially inferior. Not so, says Paul! Men and women, masters and slaves, Jews and Gentiles— all are equal in the eyes of God. Different groups of people do, however, play different and complementary roles in an orderly society.'[187] This highlights the fact that before God there is no discrimination and inequality as we are all have the same value before him as his Church. It is a shame that in our post- modern world there is still racial inequality and discrimination even among the Christians.

Guzik further draws from Jones referring to the authority of a man: ' "It is not naked power, it is not the power of a dictator or a little tyrant, it is not the idea of a man who arrogates to himself certain rights, and tramples upon his wife's feelings and so on, and sits in the home as a dictator… No husband is entitled to say that he is the head of the wife unless he loves his wife… So the reign of the husband is to be a reign and a rule of love; it is a leadership of love." (Lloyd-Jones)'[188] This means that man should not use their position to dominate and abuse women but to demonstrate love in their leadership.

Guzik elaborates on how man should love their wives: '**Love your wives**: Paul used the ancient Greek word *agape*. The ancient Greeks had four different words we translate **love**. It is important to understand the difference between the words, and why the apostle Paul chose the Greek word *agape* here.

---

[187] Charles R. *Insights on Galatians, Ephesians.*2015)284
[188] David Guzik(2021),(enduring Word Bible Commentary Ephesians)(OnlineBible Commentary) Available: https://enduringword.com/bible-commentary/Ephesians-5/ Accessed 22/02/2021

i. *Eros* was one word for love. It described, as we might guess from the word itself, *erotic* love. It refers to love driven by *desire*.

ii. *Storge* was the second word for love. It refers to family love, the kind of love there is between a parent and child or between family members in general. It is love driven by *blood*.

iii. *Philia* is the third word for love. It speaks of a brotherly friendship and affection. It is the love of deep friendship and partnership. It might be described as the highest love of which man, without God's help, is capable of. It is *fondness*, or love driven by *common interests and affection*.

iv. *Agape* is the fourth word for love.'[189]

This indicates that Paul is encouraging the husbands to love their wife as Christ loved the Church. Christ loved the Church with the agape love, the unselfish love, the love that gives without expecting anything in return, the love that is constant, the love that does not force itself to someone yet it loves even it is rejected.

Eph 6:1-9 (NKJV)

'Children, obey your parents in the Lord, for this is right."Honor your father and mother," which is the first commandment with promise:"that it may be well with you and you may live long on the earth."And you, fathers, do not provoke your children to wrath, but bring them up in the training and admonition of the Lord. Bondservants, be obedient to those who are your masters according to the

---

[189] David Guzik(2021),(enduring Word Bible Commentary Ephesians)(OnlineBible Commentary) Available: https://enduringword.com/bible-commentary/Ephesians-5/ Accessed 22/02/2021

flesh, with fear and trembling, in sincerity of heart, as to Christ; not with eyeservice, as men-pleasers, but as bondservants of Christ, doing the will of God from the heart, with goodwill doing service, as to the Lord, and not to men, knowing that whatever good anyone does, he will receive the same from the Lord, whether he is a slave or free. And you, masters, do the same things to them, giving up threatening, knowing that your own Master also is in heaven, and there is no partiality with Him.'[190] Paul honours the community protocols as he encourages each one to correctly take their rightful responsibility.

Heil further draws from Hoehner: "'The term 'children' primarily denotes relationship rather than age, and could on occasion include adult sons and daughters, who were expected to honour their parents, especially fathers, who could maintain authority in the family even until death. Here the text has in view children who are in the process of learning and growing up (cf. v. 4). . . . Children are here addressed as responsible members of the congregations. They are to 'obey' both parents, and this is a further example of the submission within divinely ordered relationships that is expected in God's new society (v. 21).'"[191] This means that parents have the right to be respected by their children even if Children have become adults. It is most common that some Christians disrespect their own parents just because they may not be of the same faith as themselves or they may have grown old. Most people suffer from dementia at their old age which makes them vulnerable to financial, physical, emotional or psychological abuse even by members of their own children and others

---

[190] Eph 6:1-9(NKJV)
[191] Heil, John Paul. 2007. *Ephesians : Empowerment to Walk in Love for the Unity of All in Christ..*2007)256

Paul goes on to encourage parents to bring up their Children in a godly way. This means that abuse can be from either side, parents or children. Paul warns fathers not to provoke their children to anger.

Swindoll further proclaims: 'The idea is that through his overbearing actions a father can push a child over the edge, not only failing to impart wisdom but actually pushing a child away from wisdom! What are some of the things that "goad" children toward anger, resentment, and bitterness? unreasonable demands for perfection constant nagging over minor infractions not leaving room for freedom of expression and personal growth lack of encouragement and affirmation harsh, unloving rebukes or cruelty public embarrassment verbal or physical abuse inconsistent discipline showing favoritism for one child over another unfair or extreme discipline that doesn't match the offense overprotective hovering that stifles growth Instead of provoking, which brings children down.'[192] This teaches us never to show favouritism for each child and never to be very strict on our children as this can lead to abuse and we may end up with a broken relationship between parents and their children. It is important to understand that Children are different individuals who have their own will and choice. Therefore parent can guide them through biblical principles in a respectful manner with the understanding that they cannot be a copy of us in terms of decision making. We need to be able to control ourselves before we even think of disciplining our Children so that we do it in the fear of God.

In his further elaboration Swindoll asserts: 'Instead of provoking, which brings children down, Paul says, "bring

---

[192] Charles R. *Insights on Galatians, Ephesians.*2015)292

them up in the discipline and instruction of the Lord" (6:4). The Greek word for "bringing up," ektrephō [1625], also appears in 5:29, referring to the nourishment of one's own flesh. So, just as husbands are to nourish their wives as they would their own bodies, fathers are to nurture their children. This includes providing for their physical, mental, emotional, and spiritual needs. It means providing proper, balanced, loving discipline when the child goes astray . . . and it means instructing the child positively in the right way. Speaking of which, a good sense of humor can add great joy in the home. Happiness is often a sign of healthy relationships. Wise are those parents who bring laughter and fun into their family work projects, mealtime discussions, and everyday conversations!'[193] This means that parents have a duty to bring up their children a proper, balanced, loving way of life. This does not make room to weak parenting skills in which parents don't have say on the life of their children. Parents should be firm in guiding their children but loving in their care.

Eph 6:10 -18

'Finally, my brethren, be strong in the Lord and in the power of His might. Put on the whole armor of God, that you may be able to stand against the wiles of the devil. For we do not wrestle against flesh and blood, but against principalities, against powers, against the rulers of the darkness of this age, against spiritual hosts of wickedness in the heavenly places. Therefore take up the whole armor of God, that you may be able to withstand in the evil day, and having done all, to stand. Stand therefore, having girded your waist with truth, having put on the breastplate of righteousness, and having shod your feet with the preparation of the gospel of peace; above all, taking the

---

[193]Charles R. *Insights on Galatians, Ephesians.*2015)292

shield of faith with which you will be able to quench all the fiery darts of the wicked one. And take the helmet of salvation, and the sword of the Spirit, which is the word of God; praying always with all prayer and supplication in the Spirit, being watchful to this end with all perseverance and supplication for all the saints.'[194]

First of all Paul encourages the Christians to be strong in the lord before putting on the armour of God. It is like when one joins the army, they require your physical fitness before you even carry the gun or put on the army uniform. When I was a pastor in at Llewellyn and Imbizo Barracks in Zimbabwe I witnessed some recruits in training before they were taken into fulltime army. Most of the young man passed out due to the heavy training. Paul is encouraging the spiritual stamina before one puts own the armour although we are already in a spiritual warfare with the enemy.. Paul begins by encouraging the believers to be strong in the power of his mighty which indicates that the strength required for the spiritual warfare is not our own physical strength but we have to subject ourselves under God's mighty power. As God revealed it to Zerubabel : Zechariah 4:6 (NIV) 'So he said to me, "This is the word of the LORD to Zerubbabel: 'Not by might nor by power, but by my Spirit,' says the LORD Almighty.'[195]

Swindoll proclaims: 'Because we fight a spiritual battle, only spiritual armor can protect us. Observe that this isn't your armor—it's God's armor. You can't provide it for yourself. You can't muster up enough mental, emotional, or physical strength to fight a spiritual battle. It's utterly impossible. Since the enemy is spiritual,

---

[194] Eph 6:10-18
[195] Zechariah 4:6 (NIV)

you and I need spiritual armor.'[196] This explains that the warfare is spiritual and that it needs a spiritual armour which God alone can provide.

Bock elaborates: ' There are forces that seek to derail those aligned to God from this path. The struggle is pictured as hand-to-hand combat.'[197] This explains that the Church is engaged in warfare with spiritual forces that aim to divert the Church from its purpose. The devil hates the purposes of God and he does all he can with his demonic forces to try and stop the purpose of God with the Church.

Bock further asserts: 'What is distinctive here is that the battle is seen as being not between people but between believers and spiritual forces (6:12). To survive, one must be prepared for this battle and engage with it at the level at which it is being fought. That means drawing on the spiritual provisions God has given us and not being focused on the circumstances. This is the most explicit 'cultural war text' we have in the New Testament epistles, but it defines that battle in ways that are distinct from most of the ways the church engages in that battle today. That is because it is the spiritual forces that are the concern. It is resisting their efforts that Paul stresses, not our material circumstances. Today's approach is often dedicated to fighting people, who actually are a goal in mission, as Paul suggests at the end of the unit.'[198] This means that the battle demands us to be spiritual as we are

---

[196] Charles R. *Insights on Galatians, Ephesians.*2015)302
[197] Bock, Darrell L. Ephesians : An Introduction and Commentary. Westmont: InterVarsity Press.2019) 197 David Guzik(2021),(enduring Word Bible Commentary Ephesians)(OnlineBible Commentary) Available: https://enduringword.com/bible-commentary/Ephesians-6/ Accessed 22/02/2021
[198] Bock, Darrell L. Ephesians : An Introduction and Commentary.2019) 197

engaging in a spiritual warfare. It is important to know that we cannot use our own ability. This demands prayer, fasting and the armour of God.

Dake elaborates on the four kinds of spirit rebels:(1) Gr- Archas, principalities, chief rulers or beings of the highest rank or order in satan's kingdom Eph 6:12,Col 2:10(2)Gr-exouusia, authorities, those who derive their power from and execute the will of the chief rulers. Eph 6:12, Col 2:10(3) Gr kosmokratopas, world rulers of darkness of this age, the spirit world rulers, Dan 10:13-21,

Eph 6:12

(4) Gr- pnuematika ponerias, spiritual wickedness,that of the wicked spirits of Satan in the heavenlies. Eph 6:12, Col 1:16-18'[199] This explains how strategic the protocol and the strategy in the kingdom of darkness where the Archas or principalities take the highest position and the Exousia or authorities take the second highest position. The Kosmokratopas or world rulers takes the third highest position and finally the Pneumatika ponerias taking the forth and list position in the kingdom of darkness. This calls the Church not to take the spiritual warfare lightly as it is well strategized against the Church. This explains that we are in a spiritual warfare as the Church and behind every evil there is a spirit of darkness that needs to be spiritually discerned and overcome. Praise be to God because our victory is in Jesus Christ who overcame the devil through his atonement sacrificial death. Colossians 2:15 (AMP) ' When He had disarmed the rulers and authorities, those supernatural forces of evil operating against us, He made a public example of them exhibiting

---

[199] Finis Jennings Dake,*Dakes Annotated Reference Bible*, (Lawrenceville, Georgia 1992) 214

them as captives in His triumphal procession, having triumphed over them through the cross.'200 This explains our victory in Christ. We do not have to fear because the victory against the evil one is already won. All we need to do is to maintain our position of submission before the lord Jesus Christ and resist the devil and he will flee away from us as James declared in James 4:7 (AMP) 'So submit to the authority of God. Resist the devil stand firm against him and he will flee from you.'[201]

Paul prescribes special armour required for this battle. He describes the spiritual armour metaphorically likening it to a well dressed Roman soldier that is ready for battle. It is possible that Paul was inspired by the prison guards who were assigned to take care of him as he was in Roman prison. Osborne asserts: 'Paul's list begins with the defensive aspects of battle. The "day of evil" has arrived, and we must "stand [our] ground," resisting the onslaughts of the enemy. Picture the scene from the movie Braveheart of the Scottish forces in the valley, waiting for the British army to arrive on the hills surrounding them. The "day of evil" has been variously understood as a general reference to the difficulties we experience in the present age (the "evil days" of 5:16), specific periods of serious persecution and trials, or the troubles of the last days centering on the "man of lawlessness" or the antichrist of 2 Thessalonians 2:3– 12 and 1 John 2:18. Likely Paul has in mind all of these and is referring to the spiritual battles of the present age that will culminate at the end of the age. As Hebrews 12:11 reminds us, all of these difficulties are painful and discouraging, but God

---

[200] Col 2:15(AMP)
[201] James 4:7 (AMP)

clothes us with his armor and makes certain it will ultimately produce "the peaceful fruit of righteousness."'[202]

Osborne helps our imagination of Paul's metaphor with his local full armed Scottish soldier from a most popular Braveheart movie of the 21st century. He gives an example of the war between the Scottish army and the British of which it is good to know that these wars led to a beautiful union of what is now the United Kingdom. But with the spiritual warfare the seems to be no reunion of the two parties as Paul affirms: 2Corinthians 6:14 (ESV) 'Do not be unequally yoked with unbelievers. For what partnership has righteousness with lawlessness? Or what fellowship has light with darkness?'[203] This explains that the kingdom of darkness can never come to an agreement but what we know is that the kingdom of God conquers and takes over the dominion. This also explains that as Christians we face the evil day always from the spiritual forces of darkness but our victory is in the lord Jesus Christ.

Paul mentions two kinds of the spiritual armour which are the offensive armour for attacking as well as the defensive armour for protection.

Dake elaborates further: Defensive armour : '(1) Gr-perikafalala, the helmet for the head and various forms embossed with many kinds of figures. (2) Gr-zoma, the girdle for the loins to brace the armour tight against the body, and support daggers, swords and other weapons. (3) Gr – thoraz, the breastplate in two parts- one to cover the breast and the other the back to protect the vital organs of the body. It extended down to the legs. (4) Gr –knemides, brazen boots for the feet to cover the front of the leg. A

---

[202] Osborne, Grant R. *Ephesians Verse by Verse*. 2017)151
[203] 2 Corinthians 6:14 (RSV)

kind of solea was often used to protect the feet from rocks, thorns, etc.(5) Gr- thureos, a shield, to protect the body from the blows and cuts.

Offensive armour: ' (1) Gr- machaira, sword, to destroy the enemy and bring his surrender. Besides the sword other weapons of offense were used – the spear, lance, battle-axe, club, bow and arrow, and sling.'204 This indicates that it was important to have both the protective and the offensive armour in order to be assured of victory. It also demonstrate that it was important to have head covered as the most important part of the body which relates the importance of our mental health as humans. It is most common today to have people suffering from mental health problems because of the stress and worries of life but with the assurance of salvation one attains tranquillity of the mind even in the midst of challenges. With the good example of the present time when people are worried about the pandemic, salvation becomes the sauce of our peace and hope for the next day. With the belt of truth in place one find a position to hang all other weapons. Jesus claims to be the way: John 14:6 (KJV) 'Jesus saith unto him, I am the way, the truth, and the life: no man cometh unto the Father, but by me.'. In this I relate the belt of truth with Jesus Christ who is the truth. We need to hang everything upon him as the scripture instructs us to cast all our cares upon the lord.

The fact that they have to put on the breastplate of righteousness is related to our imputed righteousness that comes through Christ's atonement. We are the righteousness of God in Christ who was made to be sin that we may be made the righteousness of God as in 1 Cor 5:21. We approach God with boldness and without feeling guilty as illustrated in Hebrews 4:16.

---

[204] Finis Jennings Dake,*Dakes Annotated Reference Bible*,) 214

The boots of the gospel of peace is related to the gospel and the word of God that directs our way of life as Psalm 37:23 KJV 'The steps of a good man are ordered by the Lord: and he delighteth in his way.' This may mean that we live our daily life in line with the word of God or else if we follow our own human ways we may get ourselves hurt by life experiences.

Guzik draws from Wood: 'On the shoes: "Josephus described them as 'shoes thickly studded with sharp nails'… so as to ensure a good grip. The military successes both of Alexander the Great and of Julius Caesar were due in large measure to their armies' being well shod and thus able to undertake long marches at incredible speed over rough terrain." (Wood)'205 This calls for the full preparation for a daily walk with Christ in this spiritual warfare. This comes through an intimate daily relationship with the lord. It is possible that Paul was reflecting on Isaiah 52:7 as he spoke of the shoes:(RSV) 'How beautiful upon the mountains are the feet of him who brings good tidings, who publishes peace, who brings good tidings of good, who publishes salvation, who says to Zion, "Your God reigns."'206 This encourages us to be well prepared and ready with the gospel of Jesus Christ.

The shield of faith is related to our daily Christian walk which is by faith in Jesus and not by sight as Paul proclaims in 2 Corinthians 5:7.Just as the shield is meant to protect a warrior from the fiery darts of the enemy so is

---

[205] David Guzik(2021),(enduring Word Bible Commentary Ephesians)(OnlineBible Commentary) Available: https://enduringword.com/bible-commentary/Ephesians-5/ Accessed 22/02/2021
[206] Isaiah 52:7(RSV)

our faith today. It is our faith which keeps us going on even when we feel discouraged especially during this pandemic period. This faith keeps giving us a reason to get up in the morning and face another day. We use this faith to block away all negative thoughts which may be caused by the Corona Virus experience.

Finally the sword of the spirit is the word of God which is the offensive weapon by which we attach the evil one. The writer of Hebrews proclaims in Hebrews 4:12, (KJV) 'For the word of God is quick, and powerful, and sharper than any twoedged sword, piercing even to the dividing asunder of soul and spirit, and of the joints and marrow, and is a discerner of the thoughts and intents of the heart.'[207]. This means that we declare the word of God into every situation. The devil speaks through our thoughts and we can only overcome those evil thoughts by replacing them with what the word of God says in such a situation. The devil is never afraid of any intelligent, philosophical or theological words but the word of God. This encourages us to study the scriptures and be able to use it against any circumstances of life.

Verhey, and Harvard asserts: 'In Ephesians it is clear that we need not fear the principalities and powers. The powers were regarded as intimately involved with political and social realities. They were active in the structures of human life and of the cosmos, in government and gravity, but also in received social institutions, in the "natural" arrangements of marriage and family and economy. We need not fear the powers. They have been stripped of their claims to ultimacy. They have been unmasked; the deceptions by which they nurture enmity and division have been revealed. They are not gods, but there is one!

---

[207] Hebrews 4:12 (KJV)

They do not rule, but Christ does! They have been made subject to Christ. So we can be subject to the governments and to social institutions but reject their claims to ultimacy and the enmity they nurture. We can be subject to so-called natural arrangements but qualify and adapt them and transform them into something a little more worthy of Christ's sovereignty over them.'208,.

This indicates how Verhey and Harvard relates the principalities and powers to the government and family order with its political and social realities. It is true that we need not to fear or worship our governments and family protocols although we give them our respect but to worship and honour Jesus Christ the lord.

Eph 6:18-24(YLT)

' through all prayer and supplication praying at all times in the Spirit, and in regard to this same, watching in all perseverance and supplication for all the saints and in behalf of me, that to me may be given a word in the opening of my mouth, in freedom, to make known the secret of the good news, for which I am an ambassador in a chain, that in it I may speak freely--as it behoveth me to speak. And that ye may know ye also--the things concerning me--what I do, all things make known to you shall Tychicus, the beloved brother and faithful ministrant in the Lord, whom I did send unto you for this very thing, that ye might know the things concerning us, and that he might comfort your hearts. Peace to the brethren, and love, with faith, from God the Father, and the Lord Jesus

---

[208] Verhey, Allen, and Harvard, Joseph S. *Ephesians : A Theological Commentary on the Bible.* (Louisville: Presbyterian Publishing Corporation 2011)198

Christ!The grace with all those loving our Lord Jesus Christ--undecayingly! Amen'[209].Finally in his conclusion uses prayer as another spiritual weapon against the evil one of which Paul ask the believers of Ephesus to pray for him that he may communicate the word of God with eloquence. Paul wanted to utilise his time as a prisoner in Rome to communicate the gospel to the Roman authorities. Paul took it as a privilege to be incarcerated in Rome as he had a burden for people of Rome to receive salvation. In his conclusion Paul also states another reason for his letter which was to communicate his state of being while in prison.

Verhey, Allen, and Harvard asserts further : 'As the letter had begun with "grace ... and peace," now it ends with "peace ... and grace" (6:23, 24). Together they create a kind of envelope for this message of God's blessing and our calling, for this account of the peace wrought by Christ and the peace to be performed in the church, for this proclamation in both indicative and imperative of a grace that triumphs over the cultures of enmity. The triumph of God's peace and grace is certain, even if the cultures of enmity still threaten. Even while they threaten, Ephesians promises peace and grace. And because they still threaten, Ephesians calls the church to resist the cultures of enmity, to "be strong in the Lord," and to perform God's peace and grace'[210].

This indicates that as a Hebrew tradition again Paul proclaims his benediction to the Church in Ephesus as he did in his salutation. This demonstrates how important the words of benediction are even in this present generation. It is the reflection of these words which encourage people to

---

[209] Eph 6:18-24(YLT)
[210] Verhey, Allen, and Harvard, Joseph S. *Ephesians : A Theological Commentary on the Bible* 2011)218

maintain a positive attitude even in the midst of challenges.

Conclusion and Book overview

Ephesians elucidates how the Church arrives to full spiritual maturity in Christ. The first part defines the Good News of God's doings (Eph. 1-3). The second sector provides guidelines on how to live in light of those blessings (Eph. 4-5). The book of Ephesians ends with an inspiration to stand firm in the midst of adversity (Eph. 6).

In general from the book of Ephesians, we learn on the power of the Gospel of Christ and how it can break the barriers created by culture.

Acknowledgements

I am grateful for constant inspiration, support and guidance from all the Teaching staffs of The University of West of Scotland (SBC) who helped me in effectively completing my work. Also, I would like to extend my sincere gratitude to Rev Ian Beach for his judicious support and reassurance. Above all I give all the praise and honour to the lord Jesus Christ the Father and the Holy Spirit for enabling me to write this piece of work.

Finally I speak a blessing to the Student Awards Agency Scotland (SAAS) which gave me a second chance in life.

May God bless you all.

About the author

Joseph Gilson is the senior pastor of Joy Ministries (Excellencia Global Mission) in the UK and Abroad. He is a postgraduate of University of West of Scotland and of Africa Multination for Christ University. He also studied Health and Social Care from Brooksby College in Milton Mowbray and from Leicester College. Joseph became a Bible teacher at AMFC Glenorah and AMFC Bulawayo at the same time leading a Church in Bulawayo. He became a missionary in Botswana where he was the church Overseer of the Northern Province. He relocated to UK where he was a travelling pastor planting Churches in the South East coast of England before relocating to Scotland for the purpose of planting more churches.

joe.gils71@gmail.com

00447383989122

Footnotes

Acts 24:5

[2] Margaret Aymer, Kittredge, Cynthia Briggs, and Sanchez, David A., eds. *The Letters and Legacy of Paul Fortress Commentary on the Bible.*)31

[3] Acts 19:21

[4] B.Lightfoot, J.. *Philippians.* Wheaton: Crossway. 1994)15

[5] Aida Spencer Besançon. *2 Timothy and Titus.* (Eugene: Wipf and Stock Publishers. 2014.)76

[6] David Guzik(2021),(enduring Word Bible Commentary Philippians)(OnlineBible Commentary) Available: https://enduringword.com/bible-commentary/Ephesians-1/ Accessed 24/01/2021

[7] Zondervan. *Ephesians.* (Grand Rapids: HarperCollins Christian Publishing. 2010.)33

[8] Segovia, Fernando F., and Sugirtharajah, R. S., eds. *A Postcolonial Commentary on the New Testament Writings : Postcolonial Commentary on the New Testament Writings.* (London: Bloomsbury Publishing Plc.2009)274

[9] Segovia, Fernando F., and Sugirtharajah, R. S., eds. *A Postcolonial Commentary on the New Testament Writings : Postcolonial Commentary on the New Testament Writings.* (London: Bloomsbury Publishing Plc.2009)265

[10]Segovia, Fernando F., and Sugirtharajah, R. S., eds. *A Postcolonial Commentary on the New Testament Writings : Postcolonial Commentary on the New Testament Writings.* 266

[11]West,G.O.(2008).Doing Post-colonial Biblical Interpretation@Home:Ten years of(South)African Ambivalence. *Neotestamentica, 42*(1),147–164. http://www.jstor.org/stable/43049259 accessed: 11/10/21

[12]David A Desilva. A Week in the life of Ephesus. InterVarsity Press Downers Grove, Illinois. 2020) 32

[13]Anthony Thiselton *The Living Paul : An Introduction to the Apostle's Life and Thought.* (Downers Grove: InterVarsity Press. 2010.)32

[14] Osborne, Grant R. *Ephesians Verse by Verse.* Oak Harbor: Lexham Press.2017)10

[15] Anthony Thiselton C *The Living Paul : An Introduction to the Apostle's Life and Thought.* (Downers Grove: InterVarsity Press. 2010.)33

[16]Anthony Thiselton *(The Living Paul : An Introduction to the Apostle's Life and Thought.)*34

[17]Anthony Thiselton *(The Living Paul : An Introduction to the Apostle's Life and Thought.*)35

[18]Elmer, Ian J. *Paul, Jerusalem and the Judaisers : The Galatian Crisis in Its Broadest Historical Context.*(Mohr Siebeck, Tübingen,2009)2

[19] Williamson, Peter S.. *Ephesians.* (Grand Rapids: Baker Academic.2009)41

[20] David Guzik(2021),(enduring Word Bible Commentary Ephesians)(OnlineBible Commentary) Available: https://enduringword.com/bible-commentary/Ephesians-1/ Accessed 24/01/2021

[21] 2Timothy 3:16,17

[22] Zondervan. *Ephesians.* (2010)42

[23] Ephesians 1:2

[24] .Johnson, K.L. (2017). Grace. In W.A. Elwell, Evangelical dictionary of theology. (3rd ed.). [Online]. Ada: Baker Publishing Group. Available from: https://dtl.idm.oclc.org/login?url=https://search.credoreference.com/content/entry/bpgugxt/grace/0?institutionId=8909 [Accessed 28 January 2021].

[25] Ephesians 2:9

[26] John 20:26

[27] Eph 1:3 (The Passion Translation)

[28] Thielman, Frank. *Ephesians (Baker Exegetical Commentary on the New Testament).* (Grand Rapids: Baker Academic.2010)37

[29] Psalms 103:1,2

[30] Thielman, Frank. *Ephesians (Baker Exegetical Commentary on the New Testament.*2010).37-38.

[31] Williamson, Peter S. *Ephesians.* (Grand Rapids: Baker Academic.2009)48

[32] David Guzik(2021),(enduring Word Bible Commentary Ephesians)(OnlineBible Commentary) Available:

https://enduringword.com/bible-commentary/Ephesians-1/ Accessed 04/02/2021

[33] Segovia, Fernando F., and Sugirtharajah, R. S., eds. *A Postcolonial Commentary on the New Testament Writings : Postcolonial Commentary on the New Testament Writings.* London: Bloomsbury Publishing 2009)269

[34] David Guzik(2021),(enduring Word Bible Commentary Ephesians)(OnlineBible Commentary) Available: https://enduringword.com/bible-commentary/Ephesians-1/ Accessed 04/02/2021

[35] Ephesians 1:3 (The Passion Translation)

[36] David Guzik(2021),(enduring Word Bible Commentary Ephesians)(OnlineBible Commentary) Available: https://enduringword.com/bible-commentary/Ephesians-1/ Accessed 04/02/2021

[37] David Guzik(2021),(enduring Word Bible Commentary Ephesians)(OnlineBible Commentary) Available: https://enduringword.com/bible-commentary/Ephesians-1/ Accessed 04/02/2021

[38] David Guzik(2021),(enduring Word Bible Commentary Ephesians)(OnlineBible Commentary) Available: https://enduringword.com/bible-commentary/Ephesians-1/ Accessed 04/02/2021

[39] Ephesians 1:4-5(KJV)

[40] David Guzik(2021),(enduring Word Bible Commentary Ephesians)(OnlineBible Commentary) Available: https://enduringword.com/bible-commentary/Ephesians-1/ Accessed 04/02/2021

[41] Rom 11:24(NIV)

[42] Bray, Gerald L., ed. Galatians, Ephesians. Downers Grove: InterVarsity Press.2011)234

[43] David Guzik(2021),(enduring Word Bible Commentary Ephesians)(OnlineBible Commentary) Available: https://enduringword.com/bible-commentary/Ephesians-1/ Accessed 04/02/2021

[44] John 1:8-6(KJV)

[45] Christopher H.J.Wright,*The Mission of God* (InterVarsity Press, Illinois 2006) 372

[46] Nigel G. Wright, *Free Church, Free State*(Paternoster Press, Milton Keys 2005)3

[47] Ephesians 1:7-11 (NKJV)

[48] Juan Manuel García de Alba | S.J. *Christ Jesus.* (Tlaquepaque: ITESO.2006)212

[48] Hebrews 9:22(KJV)

[50] Juan Manuel García de Alba | S.J. Christ Jesus. (Tlaquepaque: ITESO.2006)213

[51] redemption. (2017). In M. Silva, Essential Bible Dictionary. [Online]. Nashville: Zondervan. Available from: https://dtl.idm.oclc.org/login?url=https://search.credoreference.com/content/entry/zonbible/redemption/0?institutionId=8909 [Accessed 6 February 2021].

[52] 2 Corinthians 5:2-4(TPT)

[53] Couenhoven, Jesse. *Predestination: a Guide for the Perplexed.*(London: Bloomsbury Publishing Plc.2018)2

[54] David Guzik(2021)(enduring Word Bible Commentary Ephesians)(OnlineBible Commentary) Available: https://enduringword.com/bible-commentary/Ephesians-1/ Accessed 07/02/2021

[55] Bernard Lonergan: *The Redemption volume 9*, (University of Toronto Press 2018)5

[56] Bridges, Jerry. *Transforming Grace.* (Colorado Springs: NavPress Publishing Group.2017)14

[57] Matera, Frank J. *Preaching Romans : Proclaiming God's Saving Grace.* (Collegeville, MN: Liturgical Press 2010)23

[58] Eph 1:9-11 (NKJV)

[59] Eph 1:15-17(NKJV)

[60] David Guzik(2021),(enduring Word Bible Commentary Ephesians)(OnlineBible Commentary) Available: https://enduringword.com/bible-commentary/Ephesians-1/ Accessed 07/02/2021

[61] Eph 1:18-23 (NKJV)

[62] Treier, D.J. (2011). Wisdom. In I.A. McFarland, D.A.S. Fergusson, K. Kilby & et. al. (Eds.), Cambridge dictionary of Christian theology. [Online]. Cambridge: Cambridge University Press. Available from: https://dtl.idm.oclc.org/login?url=https://search.credoreference.com/content/entry/cupdct/wisdom/0?institutionId=8909 [Accessed 7 February 2021].

[63] revelation. (2017). In M. Silva, Essential Bible Dictionary. [Online]. Nashville: Zondervan. Available from: https://dtl.idm.oclc.org/login?url=https://search.credorefer

ence.com/content/entry/zonbible/revelation/0?institutionId =8909 [Accessed 7 February 2021].

[64] Eph 2:1-7 (NKJV)

[65] From death to life. (2013). In R. Hughes, Preaching the Word: Ephesians: the mystery of the body of Christ. [Online]. Wheaton: Crossway. Available from: https://dtl.idm.oclc.org/login?url=https://search.credoreference.com/content/entry/crossembc/from_death_to_life/0?institutionId=8909 [Accessed 7 February 2021].

[66] Eph 2:8-9(NKJV)

[67] Mcfarland, I.A. (2011). Grace. In I.A. McFarland, D.A.S. Fergusson, K. Kilby & et. al. (Eds.), Cambridge dictionary of Christian theology. [Online]. Cambridge: Cambridge University Press. Available from: https://dtl.idm.oclc.org/login?url=https://search.credoreference.com/content/entry/cupdct/grace/0?institutionId=8909 [Accessed 7 February 2021].

[68] David Guzik(2021),(enduring Word Bible Commentary Ephesians)(OnlineBible Commentary) Available: https://enduringword.com/bible-commentary/Ephesians-2/ Accessed 12/02/2021

[69] Philippians 2:12

[70] Grant Osborne, R.(Philippians Verse by Verse.) (Ashland: Lexham Press,2017)65

[71] Charles Swindoll R.. (*Insights on Philippians, Colossians, Philemon.*) (Cambridge,Carol Stream: Tyndale House 2017)49

[72] Ephesians 2:10 (NKJV)

[73] Thayer's greek lexicon, Electronic Database.2002, 2003, 2006, 2011 Biblesoft, Inc. aoanline . available:www.BibleSoft.com accessed: 10/02/2021

[74] Frank Thielman. *Ephesians (Baker Exegetical Commentary on the New Testament)*. Grand Rapids: Baker Academic.2010)142

[75] Eph 2:11-12 (NKJV)

[76] Frank Thielman. Ephesians (Baker Exegetical Commentary on the New Testament).2010)148

[77] Segovia, Fernando F., and Sugirtharajah, R. S., eds. *A Postcolonial Commentary on the New Testament Writings : Postcolonial Commentary on the New Testament Writings*. 267

[78] Segovia, Fernando F., and Sugirtharajah, R. S., eds. A Postcolonial Commentary on the New Testament Writings : Postcolonial Commentary on the New Testament Writings. 268

[79] Methodist Publishing, on behalf of the Methodist Church in Britain.March 2018.The EDI issues in the Methodist Church. Online. Available: https://www.methodist.org.uk/media/9017/edi-toolkit-6-final.pdf Accessed :12/-2/2021

[80] Zondervan. *Ephesians.* (Grand Rapids: HarperCollins Christian Publishing.2010)152

[81] Zondervan. Ephesians. (Grand Rapids: HarperCollins Christian Publishing.2010)153

[82] Segovia, Fernando F., and Sugirtharajah, R. S., eds. (*A Postcolonial Commentary on the New Testament Writings*

[83] : *Postcolonial Commentary on the New Testament Writings* 2009)270

[83] Eph 2:17-22 (NKJV)

[84] Eph 2:18 (NKJV)

[85] Segovia, Fernando F., and Sugirtharajah, R. S., eds. *A Postcolonial Commentary on the New Testament Writings : Postcolonial Commentary on the New Testament Writings*. 2009)269

[86] Roberts, Mark D. *Ephesians*.(Grand Rapids: HarperCollins Christian Publishing.2016)84

[87] David Guzik(2021),(enduring Word Bible Commentary Ephesians)(OnlineBible Commentary) Available: https://enduringword.com/bible-commentary/Ephesians-3/ Accessed 13/02/2021

[88] Eph 3:1 (NKJV)

[89] Zondervan.(*Ephesians*..2010)176

[90] Eph 3:3-7(KJV)

[91] Keener, Craig S. *Galatians : A Commentary*. (Grand Rapids: Baker Academic.2019)174

[92] Eph 3:8-9(NKJV)

[93] Osborne, Grant R. *Ephesians Verse by Verse*. (Oak Harbor: Lexham Press.2017)

[94] Osborne, Grant R. *Ephesians Verse by Verse*. 64

[95] Osborne, Grant R. Ephesians Verse by Verse. 64

[96] Col 2:15 (AMP)

[97] Eph 3:12(KJV)

[98] David Guzik(2021),(enduring Word Bible Commentary Ephesians)(OnlineBible Commentary) Available: https://enduringword.com/bible-commentary/Ephesians-3/ Accessed 13/02/2021

[99] David Guzik(2021),(enduring Word Bible Commentary Ephesians)(OnlineBible Commentary) Available: https://enduringword.com/bible-commentary/Ephesians-3/ Accessed 13/02/2021

[100] Acts 4:31 (AMP)

[101] Acts 5:29 (TPT)

[102] Eph 3:13(NKJV)

[103] Eph 3:14-17(NKJV)

[104] Osborne, Grant R. Ephesians Verse by Verse. 65

[105] Cohick, Lynn H.. 2010. Ephesians. Eugene: Wipf and Stock Publishers.2010)94

[106] Thielman, Frank S., Baugh, Steven M., and Arnold, Clinton E. *Ephesians, Philippians, Colossians, Philemon.* Grand Rapids: HarperCollins Christian Publishing.2015)61

[107] Eph 3:18-19 (NKJV)

[108] Roberts, Mark D. *Ephesians.* (Grand Rapids: HarperCollins Christian Publishing.2016)104

[109] Eph 3:20-21(NKJV)

[110] Able. (2016). In Editors of the American Heritage Dictionaries (Ed.), The American Heritage (R) dictionary

of the English language. (6th ed.). [Online]. Boston: Houghton Mifflin. Available from: https://dtl.idm.oclc.org/login?url=https://search.credoreference.com/content/entry/hmdictenglang/able/0?institutionId=8909 [Accessed 13 February 2021].

[111] Eph 4:1-3(NKJV)

[112] Bray, Gerald L., ed. *Galatians, Ephesians.* (Downers Grove: InterVarsity Press.2011)327

[113] Chapter 4. (2012). In F. Bruce, *The epistle to the ephesians.* [Online]. Nashville: Kingsley Books, Inc. Available from: https://dtl.idm.oclc.org/login?url=https://search.credoreference.com/content/entry/ccltdepistle/chapter_4/0?institutionId=8909 [Accessed 19 February 2021].

[114] Osborne, Grant R.*Ephesians Verse by Verse.* (Oak Harbor: Lexham Press.2017)76

[115] Osborne, Grant R.*Ephesians Verse by Verse.* 76,77

[116] Osborne, Grant R.*Ephesians Verse by Verse.* 77

[117] White, R.E. (2017). Humility. In W.A. Elwell, Evangelical dictionary of theology. (3rd ed.). [Online]. Ada: Baker Publishing Group. Available from: https://dtl.idm.oclc.org/login?url=https://search.credoreference.com/content/entry/bpgugxt/humility/0?institutionId=8909 [Accessed 14 February 2021].

[118] Osborne, Grant R.*Ephesians Verse by Verse.* 77

[119] Patience. (2003). In Collins dictionary of quotations. (2nd ed.). [Online]. London: Collins. Available from: https://dtl.idm.oclc.org/login?url=https://search.credorefer

ence.com/content/entry/hcdquot/patience/0?institutionId=8909 [Accessed 14 February 2021].

[120] Osborne, Grant R. *Ephesians Verse by Verse.* 77

[121] Eph 4:3-6

[122] Tenney, Merrill C., and Douglas, J. D. Zondervan Illustrated Bible Dictionary. Grand Rapids: HarperCollins Christian Publishing.2011)1497

[123] 1 Cor 2:4(AMPC)

[124] Osborne, Grant R. *Ephesians Verse by Verse.* (2017)82

[125] Osborne, Grant R. Ephesians Verse by Verse. (2017)82

[126] Osborne, Grant R. Ephesians Verse by Verse. (2017)82

[127] Foulkes, Francis. *Ephesians.* Illinois: (InterVarsity Press.2008)124

[128] Gordon, M.J. (2016). apostles. In J.G. Melton, Encyclopedia of world religions: Encyclopedia of Protestantism. (2nd ed.). [Online]. New York: Facts On File. Available from: https://dtl.idm.oclc.org/login?url=https://search.credoreference.com/content/entry/fofecvt/apostles/0?institutionId=8909 [Accessed 17 February 2021].

[129] Foulkes, Francis. *Ephesians* 2008)125

[130] Foulkes, Francis. *Ephesians* 2008)126

[131] Jere 3:15(NIV)

[132] 2 Tim 2:15(AMPC)

[133]Prophets and prophecy. (2002). In G. Wigoder, F. Skolnik & S. Himelstein (Eds.), The new encyclopedia of Judaism. (2nd ed.). [Online]. New York: New York University Press. Available from: https://dtl.idm.oclc.org/login?url=https://search.credoreference.com/content/entry/nyupencyjud/prophets_and_prophecy/0?institutionId=8909 [Accessed 15 February 2021].

[134]Prophet. (2006). In J. Ayto, Word origins. (2nd ed.). [Online]. London: A&C Black. Available from: https://dtl.idm.oclc.org/login?url=https://search.credoreference.com/content/entry/acbwordorig/prophet/0?institutionId=8909 [Accessed 17 February 2021].

[135]Eph 4:13-16(NKJV)

[136]Chapter 4. (2012). In F. Bruce, *The epistle to the ephesians*. [Online]. Nashville: Kingsley Books, Inc. Available from: https://dtl.idm.oclc.org/login?url=https://search.credoreference.com/content/entry/ccltdepistle/chapter_4/0?institutionId=8909 [Accessed 19 February 2021].

[137]Chapter 4. (2012). In F. Bruce, *The epistle to the ephesians*. [Online]. Nashville: Kingsley Books, Inc. Available from: https://dtl.idm.oclc.org/login?url=https://search.credoreference.com/content/entry/ccltdepistle/chapter_4/0?institutionId=8909 [Accessed 19 February 2021].

[138]Chapter 4. (2012). In F. Bruce, *The epistle to the ephesians*. [Online]. Nashville: Kingsley Books, Inc. Available from: https://dtl.idm.oclc.org/login?url=https://search.credorefer

ence.com/content/entry/ccltdepistle/chapter_4/0?institutionId=8909 [Accessed 19 February 2021].

[139] Chapter 4. (2012). In F. Bruce, *The epistle to the ephesians*. [Online]. Nashville: Kingsley Books, Inc. Available from: https://dtl.idm.oclc.org/login?url=https://search.credoreference.com/content/entry/ccltdepistle/chapter_4/0?institutionId=8909 [Accessed 19 February 2021].

[140] David Guzik(2021),(enduring Word Bible Commentary Ephesians)(OnlineBible Commentary) Available: https://enduringword.com/bible-commentary/Ephesians-4/ Accessed 17/02/2021

[141] Bray, Gerald L., ed. *Galatians, Ephesians*. (Downers Grove: InterVarsity Press.2011)343

[142] Eph 4:17-19(NKJV)

[143] Chapter 4. (2012). In F. Bruce, *The epistle to the ephesians*. [Online]. Nashville: Kingsley Books, Inc. Available from: https://dtl.idm.oclc.org/login?url=https://search.credoreference.com/content/entry/ccltdepistle/chapter_4/0?institutionId=8909 [Accessed 19 February 2021].

[144] Chapter 4. (2012). In F. Bruce, *The epistle to the ephesians*. [Online]. Nashville: Kingsley Books, Inc. Available from: https://dtl.idm.oclc.org/login?url=https://search.credoreference.com/content/entry/ccltdepistle/chapter_4/0?institutionId=8909 [Accessed 19 February 2021].

[145]Osborne, Grant R. *Ephesians Verse by Verse*. (Oak Harbor: Lexham Press.2017)93

[146] Osborne, Grant R. *Ephesians Verse by Verse*. (Oak Harbor: Lexham Press.2017)94

[147]Bray, Gerald L., ed. *Galatians, Ephesians.* (Downers Grove: InterVarsity Press.2011) 351

[148]Luke 13:3 (AMP)

[149] Mounce, William D., and Zondervan Staff. *Mounce's Complete Expository Dictionary of Old and New Testament Words.* (Grand Rapids: HarperCollins Christian Publishing 2006)800

[150]Chapter 4. (2012). In F. Bruce, *The epistle to the ephesians*. [Online]. Nashville: Kingsley Books, Inc. Available from: https://dtl.idm.oclc.org/login?url=https://search.credoreference.com/content/entry/ccltdepistle/chapter_4/0?institutionId=8909 [Accessed 19 February 2021].

[151]Eph 4:24-32 (NKJV)

[152]Chapter 4. (2012). In F. Bruce, *The epistle to the ephesians*. [Online]. Nashville: Kingsley Books, Inc. Available from: https://dtl.idm.oclc.org/login?url=https://search.credoreference.com/content/entry/ccltdepistle/chapter_4/0?institutionId=8909 [Accessed 19 February 2021].

[153]Chapter 4. (2012). In F. Bruce, *The epistle to the ephesians*. [Online]. Nashville: Kingsley Books, Inc.

Available from: https://dtl.idm.oclc.org/login?url=https://search.credoreference.com/content/entry/ccltdepistle/chapter_4/0?institutionId=8909 [Accessed 19 February 2021].

[154] Bray, Gerald L., ed. *Galatians, Ephesians.* (Downers Grove: InterVarsity Press.2011)356

[155] Bray, Gerald L., ed. *Galatians, Ephesians.* (Downers Grove: InterVarsity Press.2011)356

[156] Eph 4:29(NKJV)

[157] Chapter 4. (2012). In F. Bruce, *The epistle to the ephesians.* [Online]. Nashville: Kingsley Books, Inc. Available from: https://dtl.idm.oclc.org/login?url=https://search.credoreference.com/content/entry/ccltdepistle/chapter_4/0?institutionId=8909 [Accessed 19 February 2021].

[158] Eph 4:30 (NkJV)

[159] Chapter 4. (2012). In F. Bruce, *The epistle to the ephesians.* [Online]. Nashville: Kingsley Books, Inc. Available from: https://dtl.idm.oclc.org/login?url=https://search.credoreference.com/content/entry/ccltdepistle/chapter_4/0?institutionId=8909 [Accessed 19 February 2021].

[160] Eph 4:31 (YLT)

[161] Eph 4:32(YLT)

[162] Chapter 4. (2012). In F. Bruce, *The epistle to the ephesians*. [Online]. Nashville: Kingsley Books, Inc. Available from: https://dtl.idm.oclc.org/login?url=https://search.credoreference.com/content/entry/ccltdepistle/chapter_4/0?institutionId=8909 [Accessed 19 February 2021].

[163] Thielman, Frank. *Ephesians* (Baker Exegetical Commentary on the New Testament). Grand Rapids: Baker Academic.2010)324.

[164] Mounce, William D., and Zondervan Staff. Mounce's *Complete Expository Dictionary of Old and New Testament Words*. (Grand Rapids: HarperCollins Christian Publishing.2006)498

[165] Swindoll, Charles R. *Insights on Galatians, Ephesians*. (Carol Stream: Tyndale House Publishers. 2015)265

[166] Eph 5:2(NKJV)

[167] Eph 5:3-5(NKJV)

[168] Heil, John Paul. 2007. Ephesians : Empowerment to Walk in Love for the Unity of All in Christ. Atlanta: Society of Biblical Literature.

[169] Eph 5:3-5(AMP)

[170] Swindoll, Charles R.. *Insights on Galatians, Ephesians*. Carol Stream: Tyndale House Publishers. 2015)266

[171] Eph 5:6-7(AMP)

[172] Swindoll, Charles R. *Insights on Galatians, Ephesians*.2015)267

[173] Eph 5:8-13(YLT)

[174] Swindoll, Charles R. *Insights on Galatians, Ephesians*.2015)271

[175] Matt 5:14-16(RSV)

[176] Eph 5:14-17(RSV)

[177] Swindoll, Charles R. *Insights on Galatians, Ephesians*.2015)272

[178] Proverbs 24:16(AMP)

[179] Eph 5:10-21(YLT)

[180] Swindoll, Charles R. *Insights on Galatians, Ephesians*.2015)278

[181] Eph 5:22-33(NKJV)

[182] Heil, John Paul. Ephesians : *Empowerment to Walk in Love for the Unity of All in Christ*. Atlanta: Society of Biblical Literature.2007)241

[183] Charles R. *Insights on Galatians, Ephesians*.2015)283

[184] David Guzik(2021),(enduring Word Bible Commentary Ephesians)(OnlineBible Commentary) Available: https://enduringword.com/bible-commentary/Ephesians-5/ Accessed 22/02/2021

[185] Heil, John Paul. Ephesians : *Empowerment to Walk in Love for the Unity of All in Christ*. Atlanta: Society of Biblical Literature 2007)246

[186] Charles R. *Insights on Galatians, Ephesians*.2015)284

[187] David Guzik(2021),(enduring Word Bible Commentary Ephesians)(OnlineBible Commentary) Available: https://enduringword.com/bible-commentary/Ephesians-5/ Accessed 22/02/2021

[188] David Guzik(2021),(enduring Word Bible Commentary Ephesians)(OnlineBible Commentary) Available: https://enduringword.com/bible-commentary/Ephesians-5/ Accessed 22/02/2021

[189] Eph 6:1-9(NKJV)

[190] Heil, John Paul. 2007. *Ephesians : Empowerment to Walk in Love for the Unity of All in Christ..*2007)256

[191] Charles R. *Insights on Galatians, Ephesians.*2015)292

[192] Charles R. *Insights on Galatians, Ephesians.*2015)292

[193] Eph 6:10-18

[194] Zechariah 4:6 (NIV)

[195] Charles R. *Insights on Galatians, Ephesians.*2015)302

[196] Bock, Darrell L. Ephesians : An Introduction and Commentary. Westmont: InterVarsity Press.2019) 197 David Guzik(2021),(enduring Word Bible Commentary Ephesians)(OnlineBible Commentary) Available: https://enduringword.com/bible-commentary/Ephesians-6/ Accessed 22/02/2021

[197] Bock, Darrell L. Ephesians : An Introduction and Commentary.2019) 197

[198] Finis Jennings Dake,*Dakes Annotated Reference Bible*, (Lawrenceville, Georgia 1992) 214

[199] Col 2:15(AMP)

[200] James 4:7 (AMP)

Osborne, Grant R. *Ephesians Verse by Verse.* 2017)151

[201] 2 Corinthians 6:14 (RSV)

[202] Finis Jennings Dake,*Dakes Annotated Reference Bible*,) 214

[203] David Guzik(2021),(enduring Word Bible Commentary Ephesians)(OnlineBible Commentary) Available: https://enduringword.com/bible-commentary/Ephesians-5/ Accessed 22/02/2021

[204] Isaiah 52:7(RSV)

[205] Hebrews 4:12 (KJV)

[206] Verhey, Allen, and Harvard, Joseph S. *Ephesians : A Theological Commentary on the Bible*. (Louisville: Presbyterian Publishing Corporation 2011)198

[207] Eph 6:18-24(YLT)

[208] Verhey, Allen, and Harvard, Joseph S. *Ephesians : A Theological Commentary on the Bible* 2011)218

Bibliography

Able. (2016). In Editors of the American Heritage Dictionaries (Ed.), The American Heritage (R) dictionary of the English language. (6th ed.). [Online]. Boston: Houghton Mifflin. Available from: https://dtl.idm.oclc.org/login?url=https://search.credoreference.com/content/entry/hmdictenglang/able/0?institutionId=8909 [Accessed 13 February 2021].

Allen Verhey, and Joseph Harvard S. *Ephesians : A Theological Commentary on the Bible*. (Louisville: Presbyterian Publishing Corporation 2011)198

Aymer Margaret , Briggs Kittredge, Cynthia , and Sanchez, David A., eds. *The Letters and Legacy of Paul Fortress Commentary on the Bible*.)31

Besancon Aida Spencer. *2 Timothy and Titus*. (Eugene: Wipf and Stock Publishers. 2014.)76

Bray, Gerald L., ed. *Galatians, Ephesians*. (Downers Grove: InterVarsity Press.2011)356

Bock, Darrell L. Ephesians : An Introduction and Commentary. Westmont: InterVarsity Press.2019) 197

Bridges, Jerry. *Transforming Grace*. (Colorado Springs: NavPress Publishing Group.2017)14

Cohick, Lynn H.. 2010. Ephesians. Eugene: Wipf and Stock Publishers.2010)94

Couenhoven, Jesse. *Predestination: a Guide for the Perplexed*.(London: Bloomsbury Publishing Plc.2018)2

Desilva David A . A Week in the life of Ephesus. InterVarsity Press Downers Grove, Illinois. 2020) 32

Elmer, Ian J. *Paul, Jerusalem and the Judaisers : The Galatian Crisis in Its Broadest Historical Context*.(Mohr Siebeck, Tübingen,2009)2

Frank Matera J. *Preaching Romans : Proclaiming God's Saving Grace*. (Collegeville, MN: Liturgical Press 2010)23

Fernando Segovia, F., and Sugirtharajah, R. S., eds. *A Postcolonial Commentary on the New Testament Writings : Postcolonial Commentary on the New Testament Writings*. (London: Bloomsbury Publishing Plc.2009)274

Finis Jennings Dake,*Dakes Annotated Reference Bible*, (Lawrenceville, Georgia 1992) 214

Garcia de Alba Juan Manuel | S.J. *Christ Jesus*. (Tlaquepaque: ITESO.2006)212

Grant Osborne, R. *Ephesians Verse by Verse*. Oak Harbor: Lexham Press.2017)10

Guzik David(2021),(enduring Word Bible Commentary Philippians)(OnlineBible Commentary) Available: https://enduringword.com/bible-commentary/Ephesians-1/ Accessed 24/01/2021

://dtl.idm.oclc.org/login?url=https://search.credoreference.com/content/entry/fofecvt/apostles/0?institutionId=8909 [Accessed 17 February 2021].

Heil, John Paul. 2007. Ephesians : Empowerment to Walk in Love for the Unity of All in Christ. Atlanta: Society of Biblical Literature.

Prophets and prophecy. (2002). Himelstein S. , Wigoder G and Skolnik F (Eds.) The new encyclopedia of Judaism. (2nd ed.). [Online]. New York: New York University Press. Available from: https://dtl.idm.oclc.org/login?url=https://search.credoreference.com/content/entry/nyupencyjud/prophets_and_prophecy/0?institutionId=8909 [Accessed 15 February 2021].

From death to life. (2013). Hughes R, Preaching the Word: Ephesians: the mystery of the body of Christ. [Online]. Wheaton: Crossway. Available from: https://dtl.idm.oclc.org/login?url=https://search.credoreference.com/content/entry/crossembc/from_death_to_life/0?institutionId=8909 [Accessed 7 February 2021].

K.L.Johnson, (2017). Grace. In W.A. Elwell, Evangelical dictionary of theology. (3rd ed.). [Online]. Ada: Baker Publishing Group. Available from: https://dtl.idm.oclc.org/login?url=https://search.credoreference.com/content/entry/bpgugxt/grace/0?institutionId=8909 [Accessed 28 January 2021].

Keener, Craig S. *Galatians : A Commentary*. (Grand Rapids: Baker Academic.2019)174

Kitzler Peter. *From 'Passio Perpetuae' to 'Acta Perpetuae' : Recontextualizing a Martyr Story in the Literature of the Early Church*. (Berlin/Boston: De Gruyter, Inc. 2015)42

Lightfoot, J .B *Philippians*. Wheaton: Crossway. 1994)15

Lonergan Bernard: *The Redemption volume 9*, (University of Toronto Press 2018)5

redemption. (2017). M. Silva, Essential Bible Dictionary. [Online]. Nashville: Zondervan. Available from: https://dtl.idm.oclc.org/login?url=https://search.credoreference.com/content/entry/zonbible/redemption/0?institutionId=8909 [Accessed 6 February 2021].

Mcfarland, I.A. (2011). Grace. In I.A. McFarland, D.A.S. Fergusson, K. Kilby & et. al. (Eds.), Cambridge dictionary of Christian theology. [Online]. Cambridge: Cambridge University Press. Available from: https://dtl.idm.oclc.org/login?url=https://search.credorefer

ence.com/content/entry/cupdct/grace/0?institutionId=8909 [Accessed 7 February 2021].

M.J.Gordon, (2016). apostles. In J.G. Melton, Encyclopedia of world religions: Encyclopedia of Protestantism. (2nd ed.). [Online]. New York: Facts On File. Available from: https://dtl.idm.oclc.org/login?url=https://search.credoreference.com/content/entry/fofecvt/apostles/0?institutionId=8909 [Accessed 17 February 2021].

Mounce, William D., and Zondervan Staff. *Mounce's Complete Expository Dictionary of Old and New Testament Words.* (Grand Rapids: HarperCollins Christian Publishing 2006)800

Patience. (2003). In Collins dictionary of quotations. (2nd ed.). [Online]. London: Collins. Available from: https://dtl.idm.oclc.org/login?url=https://search.credoreference.com/content/entry/hcdquot/patience/0?institutionId=8909 [Accessed 14 February 2021].

Prophet. (2006). In J. Ayto, Word origins. (2nd ed.). [Online]. London: A&C Black. Available from: https://dtl.idm.oclc.org/login?url=https://search.credoreference.com/content/entry/acbwordorig/prophet/0?institutionId=8909 [Accessed 17 February 2021].
2021].

Roberts, Mark D. *Ephesians.* (Grand Rapids: HarperCollins Christian Publishing.2016)104

Swindoll, Charles R. Insights on Galatians, Ephesians. (Carol Stream: Tyndale House Publishers. 2015)265

Thayer's greek lexicon, Electronic Database.2002, 2003, 2006, 2011 Biblesoft, Inc. aoanline . available:www.BibleSoft.com accessed: 10/02/2021

Thiselton Anthony *The Living Paul : An Introduction to the Apostle's Life and Thought.* (Downers Grove: InterVarsity Press. 2010.)32

Thielman Frank. *Ephesians (Baker Exegetical Commentary on the New Testament).* Grand Rapids: Baker Academic.2010)142

Treier, D.J. (2011). Wisdom. In I.A. McFarland, D.A.S. Fergusson, K. Kilby & et. al. (Eds.), Cambridge dictionary of Christian theology. [Online]. Cambridge: Cambridge University Press. Available from: https://dtl.idm.oclc.org/login?url=https://search.credoreference.com/content/entry/cupdct/wisdom/0?institutionId=8909 [Accessed 7 February 2021].

Chapter 4. (2012). In F. Bruce, *The epistle to the ephesians.* [Online]. Nashville: Kingsley Books, Inc. Available from: https://dtl.idm.oclc.org/login?url=https://search.credoreference.com/content/entry/ccltdepistle/chapter_4/0?institutionId=8909 [Accessed 19 February 2021].

White, R.E. (2017). Humility. In W.A. Elwell, Evangelical dictionary of theology. (3rd ed.). [Online]. Ada: Baker Publishing Group. Available from: https://dtl.idm.oclc.org/login?url=https://search.credoreference.com/content/entry/bpgugxt/humility/0?institutionId=8909 [Accessed 14 February 2021].

West, G. O. (2008). Doing Postcolonial Biblical Interpretation @Home: Ten years of (South) African Ambivalence. *Neotestamentica*, *42*(1),147–164. http://www.jstor.org/stable/43049259 accessed: 11/10/21

Williamson, Peter S.. *Ephesians*. (Grand Rapids: Baker Academic.2009)41

Wright Nigel G, *Free Church, Free State*(Paternoster Press, Milton Keys 2005)3

ZondervanJ.D ,Tenney, Merrill C., and Douglas, Illustrated Bible Dictionary. Grand Rapids: HarperCollins Christian Publishing.2011)1497

Printed in Great Britain
by Amazon